D0568985

DESIGN THINKING

for STRATEGIC

INNOVATION

DESIGN THINKING

for STRATEGIC

INNOVATION

WHAT THEY CAN'T TEACH YOU
AT BUSINESS OR DESIGN SCHOOL

IDRIS MOOTEE | WILEY

Cover image: Sarah Chung
Cover & Book design: Sarah Chung, Idea Couture

This book is printed on acid-free paper.

For general information about our other products and services, please contact
our Customer Care Department within the United States at (800) 762-2974,
outside the United States at (317) 572-3993 or fax (317) 572-4002.

Wiley publishes in a variety of print and electronic formats and by print-on-
demand. Some material included with standard print versions of this book may
not be included in e-books or in print-on-demand. If this book refers to media
such as a CD or DVD that is not included in the version you purchased, you may
download this material at http://booksupport.wiley.com. For more information
about Wiley products, visit www.wiley.com.

ISBN 978-1-118-62012-0 (cloth); ISBN 978-1-118-74885-5 (ebk);
ISBN 978-1-118-74868-8 (ebk)

Printed in the United States of America

10 9 8 7 6

To A. Mootee

Thank you, Dad, for believing in me before I did.
And you were always right.

CONTENTS

ACKNOWLEDGMENTS

This book would not have been possible without the generous help and support from a great many people. Four in particular stand out: Dr. Moran Gerard, who came to the rescue on the week before I needed to submit my final manuscript and has been a valuable colleague, friend, and editor; Sarah Chung, who has been working with me to shape the design of this book and is responsible for giving it a personality and making it awesome; Erik Roth, who took the time from his crazy schedule to write the introduction for this book; and Brian Kenet, who invited me to design and teach the Design Thinking Executive Program at the Harvard Graduate School of Design, which this book was based upon.

I owe a huge debt of gratitude to all my friends and clients around the world who provided me the opportunities to introduce these ideas to their organizations. Scott Danielson for his friendship, enlightening dialogues, and creative spirit that he radiates. And everyone at Idea Couture, including Cheesan Chew, Scott Friedmann, and Patrick Glinski who are with me throughout our journey of prototyping a great design thinking organization. And Jessica Tien for taking all those things off my plate so I never have to worry about them.

I would also like to thank the anonymous reviewers for their feedback on earlier drafts and in particular Ashley Perez and Jamie Farshci for their patience to read and edit my messy first draft. And all those who helped me to improve the clarity and readability of this book. Any errors, omissions, and misinterpretations remain mine.

I know every author receives support from their family, but mine has been awesome and they have been the source of inspirations and I'm so thankful. We all need inspiration and watching them I find something, truly in my heart, that strives me to reach a little higher…dig a little deeper…dream a little bigger!

I truly believe we are at an important tipping point in human and economic history. This book promotes the vision that sustainable growth can only be made possible when we synthesize concepts including natural capital, creative capital, and social capital and when all are integrated into the balance sheet. This vision of a design thinking organization is founded on the mutually reinforcing and integrated principles of efficiency, equity, and reciprocity. It is the habits of mind and strategy that often prevent today's dominant firms from reinvention.

FOREWORD

....

Our world is increasingly complex and difficult to interpret. Multiple forces—technological, regulatory, competitive, and so on—act on a given context to shape the rules of what is possible and probable. Uncovering the most valuable opportunities is increasingly challenging for innovators, especially those using a traditional tool kit. New product development processes typically churn out incremental, me-too solutions when more substantial innovation is needed to capture competitive advantage.

Delivering predictable, consistent, and meaningful value from innovation remains a top challenge for executives, but most find the challenge too difficult to crack. Instead companies essentially give up and rely on pure serendipity to stumble upon valuable "eureka" moments, while others default to various versions of a creative process with the hope that it will yield a great outcome. Although these approaches can certainly yield success, the repeatability needed by any large organization is quite low.

This book presents an alternative to the status quo, an alternative that some leading-edge companies have begun to adopt. Design thinking can weed through the uncertainty and anchor innovation on the fundamental drivers of customer behavior, their interactions with the surrounding ecosystem, their interactions with one another.

Although design thinking itself is not new, Idris presents a fresh look at the practical application of this competency within the modern enterprise seeking to improve its innovation performance. This book is not an academic exercise into the possibility of design but a pragmatic explanation of how design principles can be embedded into an organization to give it insight into valuable opportunities previously hidden from traditional ways of working.

This book presents a framework and way of working that accommodates the dynamism and uncertainty surrounding most decision making companies face today. It also shares a methodology on how to embed a new design thinking–based tool kit into a modern enterprise that will enable a new wave of collaboration, insight, and learning to improve the quality of decision making, the allocation of resources to the best opportunities, and ultimately the formation of a more consistent stream of value creation.

Idris challenges the philosophies that underpin the management regimes of the modern enterprise and offers an alternative that will allow companies to adapt to the forces that impact their internal and commercial performance.

This mode challenges the status quo and encourages:

· Flexibility over conformity
· Exploration of questions over answers
· Critical thinking over key assumptions
· Enablement of teams over organization structures
· A focus on doing over studying

An innovation-driven company must put a different set of capability at the core of its growth engine that puts both art and science into a commercial context. This requires organizational agility and a culture of learning. Design thinking can be an effective tool to enable both of these attributes to bloom within a company culture.

This book also offers a refreshing take on the need for economic viability and design to coexist in a complementary and symbiotic way. Too often is design used as an excuse for passing over economics that do not make sense. The mere aesthetic appeal of a new product or powerful emotional connection of a new service experience cannot be used to justify an unprofitable business proposition. The models presented in the following pages offer a compelling version of design that allows for the right balance of desirability, feasibility, and economic viability.

Apple, with all of its risk taking on product form, user experience, and design, also maintains a laser-like focus on cost control, efficiency, and profit. Delighting its customer at the end of the day is the engine that drives its hardware-centric business model. Without design, there would be no business model, and without the business model there would be no design.

The need for this integrative thinking has never been greater. Technology exponentially interconnects people, places, and objects in increasingly new ways. Understanding the nature of these interactions both at the physical and emotional level will be required to unlock the value of these complex relationships.

Idris sets the bar high for companies attempting to embed into their culture. However, the rewards for success as indicated seem well worth the investment.

—Erik Roth

Erik leads McKinsey's Global Innovation Practice and is a partner of the firm. He is the coauthor of *Seeing What's Next: Using the Theories of Innovation to Predict Industry Change*.

Everything has changed,
is changing, and
will continue to change.

Ever since we figured out fire, stone tools, language, and the other great innovations of early human-kind, change has been upon us. That's why they call it evolution. That the rate of change today is arguably faster than it has ever been before is probably true. Cultural theorist Paul Virilio refers to that rate—and our pursuit of a science and logic of speed—as dromology, from the Greek *dromos*, meaning "to race." For him, the speed at which change is occurring is as much about a dramatic shrinkage in space as it is of time. As our technology, transportation, communication, and other ways of being in the world become increasingly fast and efficient, the old traditions around which cultures, economies, and politics have been organized are upended.

One result of that speed is disruption. And few, if any, of the old traditions have been more disrupted in recent years than big business. In response to constant cultural turbulence and its effect on their reputation, growth, and bottom line, some large companies have turned to design thinking as a way to help them make sense of disruption and sustain competitiveness.

The sources of disruption are many, but one is obvious. As technological innovation accelerates, people, communities, organizations, and objects are more interconnected than ever before. Thanks to everything Internet, our world has shrunk and we are now very close. As a result, we talk more, share more, complain more, celebrate more, ideate more, and expect more.

This disruption has not been kind to businesses used to operating by the rules of the old model. We don't have to watch their TV ads anymore. We don't believe their marketing hype anymore. We don't want to eat their junk ingredients anymore. We don't have to buy from stores anymore. And we don't want the best of them to just be profit machines anymore. We want more, when we want it, how we want it, and at the price we want.

It is a vibrant and definite sea change from the way business was always done, when financial profit was a driving force. Today, people are not afraid to say, Screw business as usual!—and show they mean it.

—Richard Branson

For businesses that have been most affected by recent disruptions in technology and social communication, the challenge is one of management. Originally, management was designed for a very different set of business needs: ensuring that repetitive tasks were completed, improving economic efficiency, and maximizing labor and machine productivity. Today those needs are vastly different. Why? Because we're facing a crisis. Actually, we're facing many crises. There are crises of competition, economy, disruptive technology, job creation, social development, and sustainability. Some are more pressing than others. The natural resources crisis is certainly more pressing than the economic crisis, and it's getting worse as populations and their level of consumption keep growing faster than human and technological innovation can find ways of expanding what can be extracted from or produced in the natural world.

But there is also a crisis of trust and credibility. The management solutions that many leaders apply in case of emergency no longer cut it. With most overwhelmed by the complexity and scale of the problems that confront them, the true risk exposure of any organization is very difficult to assess. As a result, proven management tools and techniques are being questioned for their validity and effectiveness. Most were designed for a very different world and operate based on organizational designs well beyond their best-before date, like those pointless mission statements that are supposed to align employees. If you've ever wondered where such inspirational tomes originated from and what we're supposed to do with them, now might be the time to hang them on a wall and call them antiques. Or just have a laugh with Dilbert cartoonist Scott Adams, who defined a mission statement as "a long, awkward sentence that demonstrates management's inability to think properly."

We need a new way, one that's smart, human, cultural, social, and agile and that puts innovation at the core of every move it makes. That way could be design thinking. They won't teach you this at B-school or D-school, largely because these organizations suffer from the same strain of anticomplexity that haunts many big businesses. **And that's what this book is all about.**

WE WANT MORE, WHEN WE WANT IT, HOW WE WANT IT, AND AT THE PRICE WE WANT.

Quid

THE BUTTERFLY EFFECT AND LONG-RANGE PLANNING

We agree that our world is changing rapidly. The future is not like the past. The way we do business today will not be the way we do it in the future. And it's as difficult to predict the weather over the next 12 months as to predict the performance of a business.

Of course, we know that we can't *really* predict the weather. Meteorologists predict changes in weather patterns by studying atmospheric patterns, compiling data, and applying what they see to predict what they think will occur. But their record of accuracy is poor beyond the short term, largely because they are relying on the present to imagine the future. In the 1960s MIT professor, mathematician, and meteorologist Edward Lorenz formulated a model of the way air moves around the atmosphere, measuring changes in temperature, pressure, and velocity. Stripping the weather down to 12 differential equations, working through reams of printed numbers, and plotting simple charts, he discovered that slight differences in one variable could have a profound impact on the outcome of an entire system. By modeling weather, Lorenz discovered not only the fundamental mechanism of deterministic chaos—sensitive dependence on initial conditions or the "butterfly effect"—but also that long-term weather forecasting was impossible.

Similarly, much of what we do in business strategy and planning is an attempt to predict the future based on the present and the past. Despite pouring millions of dollars into enterprise resource planning systems, however, we can only project three to six months into the future at best with any reasonable accuracy. Why? Because most business leaders are averse to chaos, are overly linear, and are disconnected from global ripples not directly related to the world of business.

We are all more connected than we know.
Whether it's business or any other systems-level
organizational challenge, design thinking helps
us appreciate and make sense of the complex
connections between people, places, objects,
events, and ideas. This is the most powerful driver
of innovation. It's what guides long-range strategic
planning. It's what shapes business decisions that
have to be based on future opportunities rather
than past events. It's what sparks the imagination.
And it's what reveals true value.

APPLIED DESIGN THINKING IS STRATEGIC INNOVATION

Innovation management is about more than just planning new products, services, brand extensions, technological inventions, or novelties. It's about imagining, organizing, mobilizing, and competing in new ways. To do that with any degree of success, organizations should heed the words of American countercultural poet Tuli Kupferberg: "When patterns are broken, new worlds emerge."

If you think strategic planning powers strategic innovation, you're living in the old world. Design thinking powers strategic innovation. It can be used to begin at the beginning of an idea or used to unlock hidden value in existing products, services, technologies, and assets—thereby reinvigorating a business without necessarily reinventing it. A disciplined process that can result in significant economic value creation, meaningful differentiation, and improved customer experience, design thinking is by nature unorthodox. But it also holds the core capabilities behind innovation.

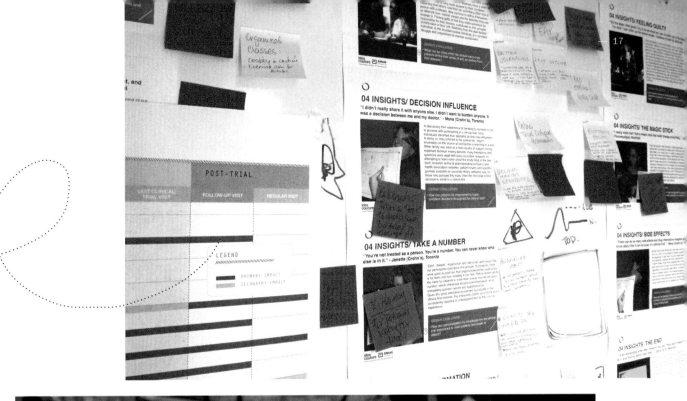

TIME TO THINK BEYOND CRISIS MODE

Sometimes we make our worst decisions when we're in the middle of a crisis. By acting reactively rather than proactively or defensively rather than offensively, we rely on how we have managed issues in the past—usually by isolating one or more discrete factors as the cause of the crisis and then attacking them. Whether it's applied in a tactical or strategic fashion, design thinking can help us get out of the crisis mode by considering challenges from a systems level.

The de facto design of management is not designed to ask managers to be creative but to deter managers from doing the wrong thing or taking extra risks.

Today, many businesses have been battered by systems-level economic failure and the collapse of traditional organizational design and management processes. These failures have left some business leaders gazing hopefully toward design thinking as the next management "wonder drug." Given how various authors have presented it as a way to address complex, ambiguous, uncertain, and volatile circumstances across multiple contexts and cultures, design thinking is often touted as bringing a refreshed, revitalized, and rejuvenated approach to management and strategic thinking. It does, but it is far from a magical cure-all. Just as the pioneers of the modernist movement recognized the need for new design concepts to match the technological advancements of the twentieth century, we need to recognize the need for new management concepts to match the disruptive era of the twenty-first century.

It has been a heady decade for design thinking. Will it fall out of favor over the next few years, like other short-lived management fads? Or will it forever change the way business is done? Only time will tell. Traditional design firms, branding agencies, and design studios are all quick to claim that they can change their clients' worlds; however, their clients might be disappointed with such a promise if their consultant partners lack an understanding of business strategy, portfolio management, market power, industry dynamics, channel economics, and capital intensity. Change requires more than just cool design and catchy slogans. Adding a few young MBAs to your staff does not turn you into a strategy consultancy firm. And brushing on a thin veneer of design thinking won't do you much better. Design Thinking is changing the paradigm of management and it will impact us for decades.

THE PROBLEM WITH THE RAT RACE IS THAT EVEN IF YOU WIN, YOU'RE STILL A RAT.

—Lily Tomlin

THE DE FACTO DESIGN OF MANAGEMENT IS NOT DESIGNED TO ASK MANAGERS TO BE CREATIVE, BUT TO DETER MANAGERS DOING THE WRONG THINGS OR TAKING EXTRA RISKS.

CHANGING MANAGEMENT PARADIGMS

20th Century $\longrightarrow$ 21st Century

20th Century	21st Century
Scale and Scope	Speed and Fluidity
Predictability	Agility
Rigid Organization Boundaries	Fluid Organization Boundaries
Command and Control	Creative Empowerment
Reactive and Risk Averse	Intrapreneur
Strategic Intent	Profit and Purpose
Competitive Advantage	Comparative Advantage
Data and Analytics	Synthesizing Big Data

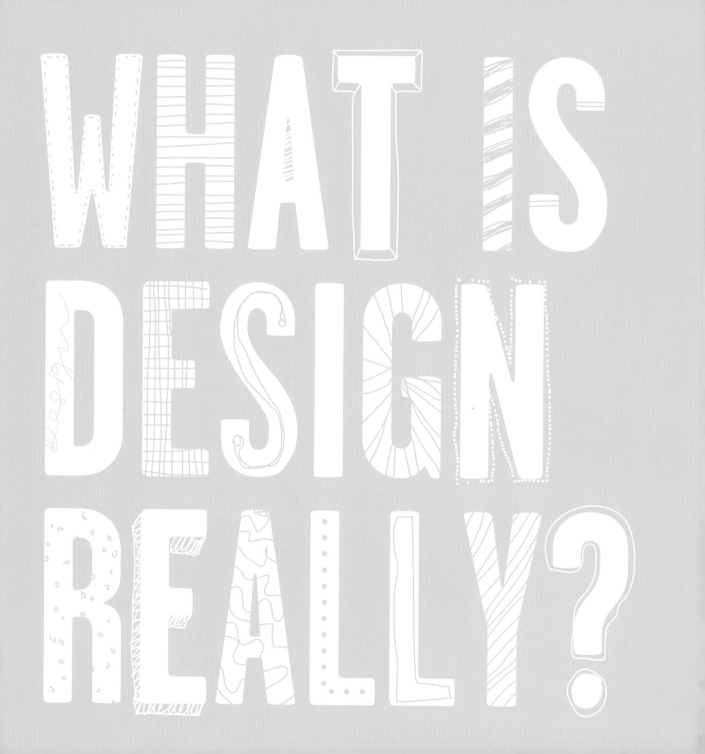

Ask a bunch of people who subscribe to design thinking exactly what it is, and you will get a bunch of answers, each of which varies just enough from the last one to give you the answer you're looking for: There is no single, unifying, common definition of *design thinking*. Given its predilection for dealing with ambiguity, perhaps there shouldn't be.

For most practitioners, the idea of design as a way of thinking can be traced backed to Herbert Simon and his 1969 book, *The Sciences of the Artificial.* An American political scientist, economist, sociologist, psychologist, and professor at Carnegie Mellon University, his distinction between critical thinking as an analytic process of "breaking down" ideas and a design-centric mode of thinking as a process of "building up" ideas is foundational to the practice. So, too, is his definition of *design* as "the transformation of existing conditions into preferred ones."

A DESIGN THINKING ORGANIZATION IS CAPABLE OF EFFECTIVELY ADVANCING KNOWLEDGE FROM MYSTERY TO HEURISTIC TO ALGORITHM, GAINING A COST ADVANTAGE OVER ITS COMPETITORS ALONG THE WAY.

From Robert McKim's 1973 book *Experiences in Visual Thinking* to Peter Rowe's first noteworthy use of the term in 1987's *Design Thinking* to Richard Buchanan's highly influential article "Wicked Problems in Design Thinking," Simon's big idea—that design is always linked to an improved future—has continued to shape the practice in every direction.

More recently, design thinking has caught the attention of businesspeople, thanks to it finding its way into the pages of publications like *Bloomberg Businessweek* and *Harvard Business Review*. Where Simon and those who followed him took a more considered, scholarly approach to the epistemological underpinnings of the practice, the understanding of design thinking in the business press is overly simplistic. In focusing on applying a human-centric approach to identifying problems followed by a rapid prototyping of ideas into tangible artifacts or nonfunctional models to solve those problems, the business press tends to do to design thinking what it does to most complex issues: turn it into an easily accessed tool kit that anyone can use.

Typically characterized as a step-by-step process that's made sexy with the help of multicolored Post-it Notes, mind maps, and other overly simplistic visual representations of complex systems or experiences, the business press has romanticized design thinking as a way to solve problems and drive profit. It's most simplistic definition? Design thinking is a way to get businesspeople to think like designers and designers to think like businesspeople. But design thinking is more than that.

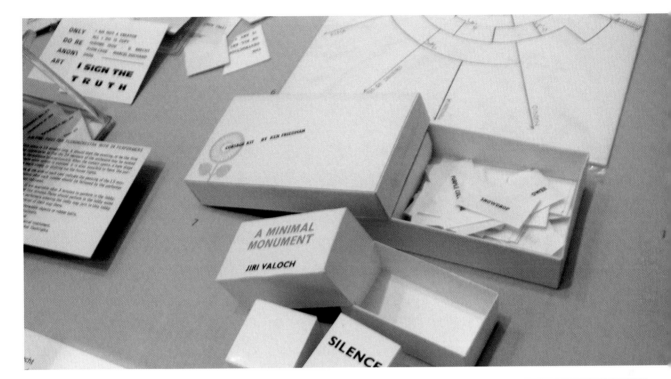

AND WITH THAT COST ADVANTAGE, IT CAN REDIRECT ITS DESIGN THINKING CAPACITY TO SOLVE THE NEXT IMPORTANT MYSTERY AND ADVANCE STILL FURTHER AHEAD OF ITS COMPETITORS.

—Roger Martin

So,
what is Design Thinking?

—— A way to take on design challenges by applying empathy?

—— An approach to collective problem solving?

—— A framework to balance needs and feasibility?

—— A means to solve complex or wicked problems?

—— A mind-set for curiosity and inquiry?

—— A fixed process and a tool kit?

—— A problem-solving approach to handle problems on a systems level?

—— A culture that fosters exploration and experimentation?

—— A design buzzword to suggest that designers can do more than just design?

—— A management buzzword sold as the next strategic tool?

The answer to all is, "Yes, and more!" Here is my definition of *design thinking*: **Design thinking is the search for a magical balance between business and art, structure and chaos, intuition and logic, concept and execution, playfulness and formality, and control and empowerment.**

In my practice, this is a framework for a human-centered approach to strategic innovation and a new management paradigm for value creation in a world of radically changing networks and disruptive technology. Although that framework is certainly populated by valuable processes or tools (which we'll get to later), it is the framework itself that is where the magical balance resides. Design thinking is about cognitive flexibility, the ability to adapt the process to the challenges. And when

it comes to organizations that successfully apply design thinking to challenges, that framework is essentially cultural. If you were to try to describe the culture of a design thinking organization, some of the words that would likely arise might include:

Human-centric	Creative and innovative
Speed and agility	Connected and flat
Adaptable and flexible	Fun and playful
Inspired	Committed
Disruptive	High-energy
Passionate	Risk-taking
Purposeful	

How many big organizations have cultures that are like this? The answer is very few, which is why innovation is so challenging without the help of other, usually smaller, organizations that do have such cultures. Respected design critic and educator Don Norman suggests that one of the major problems related to innovation is the ability to manage the desirable, feasible, and economically viable. Although he is referring to designing things, the problem is equally present when designing systems, services, or even cultures.

Design thinking is not an experiment; it empowers and encourages us to experiment.

DESIGN THINKING IS

THE SEARCH FOR

a magical balance between

BUSINESS **AND ART;**

STRUCTURE AND CHAOS;

INTUITION AND LOGIC;

CONCEPT AND EXECUTION;

playfulness and formality ; AND

~~CONTROL~~ AND <u>EMPOWERMENT</u>.

IS DESIGN THINKING A SCIENCE OR AN ART?

We don't usually associate design with science, but many design theories have been inspired by scientific disciplines, particularly the natural sciences. In such cases, design is envisioned as an objective, rational procedure that draws on the same rigorous standards of testing and verification as the sciences. These theories focus on problem framing and problem solving.

In the world of business, problems (starting point) and goals (end point) are said to be like a chess game: The initial positions of the pieces are clearly defined and the goal, of course, is to checkmate and win the game. But in design that's not the case. As Donald Schön writes in *The Reflective Practitioner*, "In real-world practice, problems do not present themselves to practitioners as givens. They must be constructed from the materials of problematic situations which are puzzling, troubling, and uncertain."

That's why design theorist and educator Horst Rittel called design problems "wicked" and proposed that we need a completely different approach, what he called a second generation of design theories and methods. He advocates that if the first generation was aiming to make design a purely rational process, the second generation recognizes that the notion of rationality implies serious paradoxes and that distinctions between systematic versus intuitive and rational versus nonrational design are untenable.

Some of the principles of design thinking originated from design discipline but were adapted to apply in a wider and more complicated business context. Design thinking is popular among educators and social entrepreneurs for social innovation because it approaches problem solving from the point of view of the end user and calls for creative solutions by developing a deep understanding of unmet needs within the context and constraints of a particular situation. Some designers are picking up the skills when working in close collaboration with other domain specialists in the field of engineering, economics, and social sciences.

It has yet to find its way into business schools so that our next generation of managers can be better equipped to handle increasingly complex challenges.

Language that used to be associated with designers has now entered other fields: Hospital administrators are told they should be more patient-centric, policy makers are told that public services should be more user-centric, and businesses engage with customers by offering new meanings for objects. Design thinking is not something that is taught and practiced in a studio anymore. For executives and managers it is becoming our everyday language.

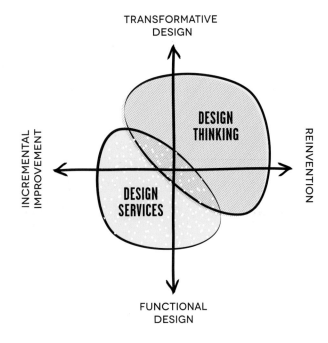

COMPLEXITY IS THE PRODIGY OF THE WORLD. SIMPLICITY IS THE SENSATION OF THE UNIVERSE. BEHIND COMPLEXITY, THERE IS ALWAYS SIMPLICITY TO BE REVEALED. INSIDE SIMPLICITY, THERE IS ALWAYS COMPLEXITY TO BE DISCOVERED.

— GANG YU

...STING

...NELIZES THE GREEN BEANS

UNTIL THEY LOSE THEIR

...VETE ENTIRELY—

THEY TURN FROM ...EN TO **BROWN**

AT **200** DEGREES C A DELICIOUS LITTLE OIL CALLED

CAFFEOL DEVELOPS. IT'S CAFFEOL THAT GIVES COFFEE MUCH OF IT'S FLAVOR & AROMA

THANKS CAFFEOL, MUCH APPRECIATED.

BEANS ARE THEN COLOUR GRADED

TO DETERMINE THEIR LEVEL OF ROAST AND FLAVOR

DARK ROASTS ARE BOLD.

LIGHTER ROASTS — COMPLEX.

THE ESPRESSO MACHINE FORCES HOT PRESSURIZED WATER THROUGH THE GROUND COFFEE AT **9** ATM

THE PRESSURE OF NINE ATMOSPHERES

NOW IT'S **COFFEE TIME**

APPLIED DES

Applied Design

THINKING

Thinking in

BUSINESS A

Business and Strategy

Applying design thinking to business problems empowers organizations and individuals within them to better understand their competitive and operational environment. From behavioral patterns to values to systems-level challenges to go-to market strategies, the process of understanding how to meet the needs of people often turns itself inward and reveals some of the deadliest organizational gaps and why they continue to persist.

In 1893 the world's first management consultant got the notion to improve industrial workflow. Frederick Taylor, aka the father of scientific management, embarked on a scientific study of industrial processes. Since the publication of Taylor's 1911 treatise, "The Principles of Scientific Management," the field of industrial engineering has attempted to improve efficiency through Taylor's management model. At almost 100 years old, scientific management is primarily based on a mechanical view of our universe as it relates to finding the "best" ways to work. Spurring powerful business models like the Ford assembly line, this discipline of speeding up productivity, controlling quality, and minimizing cost remains the primary management modus operandi.

More than 100 years later, scientists haven't made much headway in scientific management. In the mid-1980s, they turned their attention to chaos and used computer modeling to seek order through mathematical diagrams created at warp speed. Although they found some fascinating data visualizations, they couldn't explain or understand the patterns. Like forecasting the weather, all they could do was make educated predictions—never guarantee sunny skies.

A decade later, scientists turned their attention to complexity. They used advanced computer models to uncover the structure of life-forms and apply it to business. They compared everything from beehives to genetic DNA to traffic jams to the complex properties of the technological and economical environment. Although they did manage to create some compelling metaphors for strategic management, these studies fell short of revealing anything fail-proof.

THE ILLITERATE OF THE 21ST CENTURY WILL NOT BE THOSE WHO CANNOT READ AND WRITE, BUT THOSE WHO CANNOT LEARN, UNLEARN, AND RELEARN.

—Alvin Toffler

Today, Fortune 500 and other companies still manage themselves like machines, valuing profit before all else, maintaining authority with command-and-control management, and relying on Six Sigma to improve quality. They also overrely on the utilization metrics, output, and efficiency of mass production. These practices serve to create a bureaucratic structure, distance executives from customers, and encourage executives to manage rigidly and systematically.

In the language of systems thinking, the problem with modern management and its quest to ensure consistency and predictability is that it attempts to eliminate variation. Excessive variation is absolutely the enemy of predictability; indeed, the function of strategic planning, quality control, and Six Sigma is to eliminate unwanted surprises. But as we all know, there is a tendency in life, as in business, for things to become uncontrolled and go off in all directions. Innovators understand and accept this because true innovation is about maximizing the chance of lucky surprises. As such, it needs to allow some degree of variation in a somewhat purposeful fashion.

It isn't the incompetent who destroy an organization. The incompetent never get in a position to destroy it. It is those who achieved something and want to rest upon their achievements who are forever clogging things up.

—F. M. Young

The average time a chief executive officer spends in the top position is decreasing rapidly, from an average of 10 years in the 1990s to about two to three years today. The rate at which market leaders lose their leadership positions, the so-called topple rate, has doubled in the past two decades. For companies that are built to last, the average life span of an organization, irrespective of its size, is now just 12.5 years. And of all mergers and acquisitions, no more than 20 percent are actually creating value and more than 50 percent actually destroy value. In light of these facts, there are two big questions we need to ask: Is management as we know it working? and Is it time to rethink it?

Remember Herbert Simon, the guy who wrote *The Sciences of the Artificial* and introduced us all to the proto-theories of design thinking? Well, he also wrote about strategic planning and suggested that classic decision theory (and its influence on strategic planning) is useful when it comes to evaluating strategies that have already been created but not so useful when it comes to framing the problems that such strategies are meant to solve. It's even less useful when the task is generating viable strategic alternatives.

According to scenario planning expert Paul Schoemaker, the extreme emphasis on responding to new situations by extrapolating on the past is the key flaw in his discipline. New challenges have no history. Given the speed of change today, extrapolating from the past could lead companies down a dangerous path.

Another reason why most planning efforts fail is because they have "no plan behind the idea" or "no idea behind the plan." Sure, most strategic plans contain an impressive 150 pages of PowerPoint slides, but most of them are so obvious

you wonder about the value of the big idea. Those of you that have lived in this world will understand that to execute such a plan means that you need to call in the consultants to fill in the gaps. What many companies refer to as a strategic initiative isn't really that strategic and doesn't really center on an initiative. Calling something a strategic initiative doesn't make it one.

Strategy planning is predicated on the availability of information. In the past there were not enough data to support meaningful analysis. Today, it's the opposite, thanks to big data. What are big data? Typically described in terms of three key things—the volume of information (the amount from all sources), the variety of information (the nature of the information in all formats), and the velocity of information (the speed at which data are collected)—big data might be helping some companies with making smarter strategic decisions, but they are also leading those companies down the quantitative path that has made it so hard for them to design for humans in the first place.

Actually, it's a little scary. Never in the history of humankind have we produced this level of information at such speed. And it's not slowing down. As more of our daily activities are monitored and our business activities are digitized, we are coming to a point where we are suffering from data paralysis. The signal-to-noise ratio has jumped from 50 to 90 percent, and maybe 10 percent of the data is useful. Big data do not diminish the need for intuition and sense making in strategy planning; they put more demand on it. But it takes strong leadership to maintain a balanced culture when it comes to decision making.

DESIGN THINKING TO THE RESCUE

Companies find themselves in a crisis because they can't respond to change, even if they recognize the need for transformation. This is the age of extreme competition, and every competitive advantage has been reduced to comparative advantage.

Best practices are of little benefit, particularly for those looking to innovate in today's creative economy. It's getting harder to weed out problems now that we're bombarded with massive data and enterprise software that force managers to think in confining formulas. Caught in the tangle of technology, process, product portfolios, and business units, the manager's straightjacket only tightens its grip.

The relentless pursuit of growth is responsible for this chaotic cloud of debris that's made up of bygone processes, product portfolios, and data, data, data. Once we realize that more is not always better, the simple solutions hidden underneath can reveal themselves and guide the way to how to handle complex problems in new and more creative ways. This challenge and its connection to the numbers game is perhaps best summed up by Roger Martin in his book *The Design of Business*: "Data is no substitute for intimacy."

From consumers to employees to the people in a supply chain, design thinking enables teams to build more intimate relationships. It helps us eliminate the complexity and clutter so that we can get back to the basics of human needs and human problems.

Exhibi

藝 術

30/7 -1

Times Sc

代 廣

WE'VE LOST TOUCH WITH WHAT'S AROUND US

Most of the training business schools provide for managers is outdated. Much of it is grounded in false theory or theories so basic that they can be taught with PowerPoint and textbooks.

For the past 30 years, managers and consultants have been preoccupied with practicing stratagems that have nothing to do with economic value creation—constant organizational restructuring, following best practices and poorly designed growth strategies. This endless, tiresome shuffling of assets and shifting of organizational boundaries has created opportunities for investment bankers and consultants, not value for shareholders.

More than 80 percent of our management tools, systems, and techniques are for value-capture efforts, not for value creation; this includes techniques such as total quality management (TQM), enterprise resource planning (ERP), Six Sigma, Lean Startup, and Agile Systems. These tools are valuable for keeping an enterprise running smoothly. But we should be focusing on value creation rather than value capture alone. This is where design thinking comes into play. Companies such as Apple, Amazon.com, Netflix, Samsung, Burberry, and BMW are winning by design and the thinking behind that design.

One reason for the success of some leading design organizations is intuition. Intuition has the remarkable ability to bring clarity to strategic decision making because it reveals a subtle qualitative and quantitative balance that is often needed for all the parts to click. Unfortunately, it can't be taught—especially in B-school.

Sometimes we need to tune out the algorithms and the data. We need to free ourselves from the rational-logical-linear model that keeps us frozen in a fast-moving and uncertain environment. We need a touch of finesse and the courage to wipe the slate clean. We need to rely on our gut.

This might mean simplifying the amount of technology system you use while honing the innovations that truly fit your workflow. It could mean consolidating data on a knowledge-base and getting employees on the same wavelength. It could mean abolishing the command-and-control hierarchy and connecting on an egalitarian level with your company to gather new insights. It could mean reinventing your brand in a way that no brand consultant could ever do because that person doesn't own it like you do.

After so many attempts to understand industrial management as a science, there's a point when throwing in the towel, sitting back, and defaulting to your intuition will unlock the truest answers you've been seeking. Management expert Gary Hamel once said, "Management is the least efficient activity in your organization." We can make strategic management efficient only if we make it clearer. Sometimes, that clarity comes only from the inside.

EVERY FUTURE BUSINESS LEADER NEEDS TO BE A GOOD DESIGN THINKER

Applied design thinking in business problem solving incorporates mental models, tools, processes, and techniques such as design, engineering, economics, the humanities, and the social sciences to identify, define, and address business challenges in strategic planning, product development, innovation, corporate social responsibility, and beyond.

When executed correctly, this integration forms a highly productive dynamic between traditional business management approaches and design approaches, complementing and enhancing one another in a symbiotic fashion.

The adoption of multidisciplinary approaches to business problem solving, including the application of design thinking, helps organizations fill in critical gaps and deficiencies. Only by combining modes and methods can organizations establish more complete and competitive bodies of knowledge and insight that empower a human-centric, future-oriented approach. One mode is the hard management of organizational structure, reporting hierarchies, and all the usual processes. The other is the soft management systems of design thinking—the creativity, sensibility, and social bonding that truly hold an organization together. Combing these two does not discount or diminish the value of traditional or other analytical business methods in problem solving. Rather, by leveraging the best of both business and design thinking, it establishes a more sensitive, powerful, and potent analytical tool kit that escalates our thinking to a new level. This results in a holistic learning experience that is meaningful, valid, and practical to everyone involved.

THE 10 DESIGN THINKING PRINCIPLES THAT Redefine BUSINESS MANAGEMENT

· · · · · · · · ·

Design thinking helps structure team interactions to cultivate greater inclusiveness, foster creativity, deepen empathy, and align participants around specific goals and results.

Humankind has survived thus far because we can work well together, communicate, empathize, anticipate, understand, and exchange. Design thinking is a reflection of these abilities. The culture behind its practices, principles, and processes is potentially more empathetic, human-centered, and courageous than business management.

A multifunctional and multiperspective approach to solving problems has influenced many of the principles inherent in design thinking. As such, using it in business has the power to influence our core values, identities, expectations, and views of the world. But because it comes with a "responsibility to shape the future," it is critical that every new practitioner understand that it begins by acknowledging and acting upon the human need for meaning and connectivity.

Many approach design thinking as a clear-cut method because it employs some predictable and repeatable processes that can, to some extent, be codified as algorithms. But it can also embrace serendipitous, ad hoc, and adaptive approaches to inquiry, synthesis, and expression to leverage the power of intuition. As a relatively new concept to the business world, it needs to be carefully adopted and integrated into traditional management practices. It should not be exploited as a marketing tactic or used as an excuse for creative ideas to avoid analytical-based criticism or business logic. It should be positioned as a creative, logical tool that can facilitate innovation and transformation. To do this successfully, however, it is critical that organizations interested in adopting and applying design thinking recognize its key principles.

01
DESIGN THINKING IS

ACTION-
ORIENTED

· · · · · · · · ·

It proposes a cross-disciplinary learning-by-doing approach to problem solving. It allows us to accommodate varied interests and abilities through hands-on and applied learning experiences between individuals. A big part of design thinking is design doing. It's getting your hands dirty and experimenting instead of being an armchair strategist.

· · · · · · · · ·

02

DESIGN THINKING IS

COMFORTABLE

WITH CHANGE

03
DESIGN THINKING IS

Human
- C E N T R I C -

· · · · · · · · ·

It is always focused on the customer or end user's needs,
including unarticulated, unmet, and unknown needs. To do this,
design thinking employs various observational and listening-based
research techniques to systematically learn about the needs,
tasks, steps, and milestones of a person's process.

· · · · · · · · ·

04
DESIGN THINKING

INTEGRATES
FORESIGHT

05

DESIGN THINKING IS

A DYNAMIC CONSTRUCTIVE PROCESS

· · · · · · · ·

It is iterative. It requires ongoing definition, redefinition, representation, assessment, and visualization. It is a continuous learning experience arising out of a need to obtain and apply insights to shifting goals. Here, prototyping, creating of tangible sharable artifacts, becomes an important piece of the design thinking tool kit.

· · · · · · · ·

06
DESIGN THINKING

PROMOTES
EM*pathy*

07
DESIGN THINKING

REDUCES
RISKS

· · · · · · · · ·

Whether it's developing and launching a new product or a service, there are many benefits in learning from small and smart failures. This will always happen, but applied design thinking practices help reduce risks by considering all the factors in the development ecosystem, including technology, the market, competitors, customers, and the supply chain.

· · · · · · · · ·

<u>08</u>
DESIGN THINKING CAN

CREATE

MEANING

09
DESIGN THINKING CAN
BRING
Enterprise Creativity
TO
NEXT LEVEL

· · · · · · · · ·

It fosters a culture that embraces questioning, inspires frequent reflection in action, celebrates creativity, embraces ambiguity, and creates visual sense making through interactions with visualizations, physical objects, and people. A design thinking organization creates strong "inspirationalization" and "sensibility" to give tangibility to the emotional contract that employees have with organizations.

· · · · · · · · ·

10
DESIGN THINKING IS
THE *New*
"COMPETITIVE LOGIC OF BUSINESS STRATEGY"

INTRODUCI
THE DESIG
THINKING

Discontinuity is causing chaos. It's now the norm. Traditional hierarchies will not survive long. The next generation of leaders need to know how to roll with change. They also have to mobilize people who are resistant to change or don't know how to successfully adapt to an ever-evolving business environment. In this chapter we explore strategic business challenges familiar to most organizations and demonstrate how design thinking approaches can be applied to those challenges. Complex business problems today demand new leaders to manage change effectively, reinvent business models and practices rapidly enough to keep up with the competition, and outinnovate them while balancing the management of change with rapid growth.

The adaptability of any organization depends on the effective handling of other key strategic challenges: developing adaptable strategies, avoiding commoditization, creating sustaining differentiation, developing innovative culture, engaging customers and employees, responding to technological disruptions, and balancing short- and long-term strategies. For each of these business problems we apply a design thinking lens to raise new questions and shape creative ideas. Each subsection is complemented with an activity. The basic illustrative design thinking implementations serve as useful examples of how to approach business problems with empathy, creativity, foresight, and consumer-centricity. They are intended to inspire new pathways that address even the oldest and most wicked challenges. On the following pages is the list of design thinking solutions that are matched to specific business challenges.

LINKING DESIGN THINKING SOLUTIONS TO BUSINESS CHALLENGES

BUSINESS CHALLENGES 〜 **DESIGN THINKING SOLUTIONS**

Business Challenges	Design Thinking Solutions
Growth	Storytelling
Predictability	Strategic Foresight
Change	Sensing
Relevance	Value Redefinition
Extreme Competition	Experience Design
Standardization	Humanization
Creative Culture	Prototyping
Strategy and Organization	Business Model Design

Business Challenge 01

Growth

Growth is at the forefront of every business leader's mind. Most tend to utilize classic growth strategies to get there: new strategic partnerships, horizontal market expansion, vertical integration, product extension, and franchising. Although all these strategies are well known, how does an organization come to select one over the other as a means for growth? Once decided, how does a company focus its resources? And what are the implications for organizational design?

The process of redefining the boundaries of business and making explicit decisions regarding who it will and will not serve often sparks intense debates around any growth strategy. There are no simple black and white answers to these questions, but design thinking can be used to bring clarity and align its business model to achieve maximum leverage.

Philip Crosby, author of *The Eternally Successful Organization*, says growth is unavoidable "if for no other reason than to accommodate the increased expenses that develop over the years. Inflation also raises the cost of everything, and retaliatory price increases are not always possible. Salaries rise as employees gain seniority. The cost of benefits rises because of their very structure, and it is difficult to take any back, particularly if the enterprise is profitable. Therefore cost eliminations and profit improvement must be conducted on a continuing basis, and the revenues of the organization must continue to increase in order to broaden the base."

Most organizations, however, aspire to grow in order to prosper, not just survive. Growth means different things to different organizations. There are many dimensions a company can select to measure its growth.

Although the ultimate goal of most companies is profit, other financial data may be used as indications of growth. Some business leaders use revenue, EBITDA (earnings before interest, taxes, depreciation, and amortization), product line expansion, employees, or other criteria to evaluate organizational growth.

Growth is also the very essence of entrepreneurship, including corporate entrepreneurship. High growth leads to managerial complexity, so the alignment between shareholders, executive leadership, managers, and employees can quickly become choking points. Growth comes with the questions where a company's leadership, culture, systems, management, and business model can hold itself together.

Growth largely depends on increased economic activity, which requires certain preconditions, including consumer confidence and demographic shifts. The 1980s and 1990s were an unprecedented period of economic expansion in the United States as the country was driven by increasing demand for cars, housing, home appliances, and other products. The debt-fueled growth of consumer spending was boosting the gross domestic product (GDP) and creating millions of jobs while corporations were building their production capacity and pushing up their corporate profits. Growth was easy under those circumstances, and business gurus were busy selling any number of "proven" formulas to get it.

These management best practices developed during the boom period between the 1980s and 1990s were widely codified and taught in business schools around the world. They were liberally applied to industry after industry by managers trained in whatever best practice. Today, the danger lies in applying theories and practices based on those outdated models of two or three decades ago. Consider current macroeconomic trends and industry dynamics—growth is a lot harder to come by because we are operating in a very different, much more complex world. And if you're thinking about relying on emerging markets such as China, Mexico, Brazil, and India, be warned that you are entering a very different game with very different rules.

Growth can't continue unchallenged forever; our Earth's resources are finite. Sustainable growth is still a myth: It's quite impossible to decouple economic progress from environmental damage. With all of that, we are looking at a no-growth future. Unless we can reimagine and reinvent new industries, we simply cannot rely on economic growth to power our growth plan.

Growth is also the very essence of entrepreneurship, including corporate entrepreneurship.

**GROWTH NEEDS A STRATEGY, AND
EVERY STRATEGY NEEDS A STORY**

Most businesses develop specific plans
that, over time, will move their business
to a level that meets the goals of the
executive team, the shareholders, and the
investment community. The reason why
growth strategies are so vital is they keep
things moving. And in business, if you're
not going forward, you're going backward.

Growth means creating a clear and
compelling vision of the future. Your vision
needs to be very clear in terms of what
you want from your business. How do we
plan to attach an adjacency? How do we
become the market leader? How about
expanding to multiple geographies? And
what's in it for managers and employees?
Ultimately, the most meaningful yardstick
is one that shows progress with respect to
an organization's stated goals, whatever
they are. So how do you develop your
organization's stated goals? How do you
develop the vision of where you want the
organization to be in the future?

Design Thinking Approach 02

Strategic Foresight

To face the unknown, businesses must adopt a different approach to predictability. The ability to manage the uncertainties of the future is critical to planning for growth or survival. Because of the rise of the innovation society, new technologies, and a rapidly globalizing economy, business leaders are forced to deal with not only the speed of change but also massive new complexity, uncertainty, and paradox on a global scale. The future will emerge from a constant stream of decisions, strategies, and commitments that have to be made in the present, with as much understanding of risk, possibility, and wisdom as possible.

Most managers appreciate and understand the value of strategic foresight but don't know how to make it tangible enough or integrate it into business strategy. Strategic foresight is not "planning"; it's one of the many inputs for planning. Strategic planning needs to consider a multitude of factors in the present competitive and operational environment and then extrapolate the data into a possible future that is based on a rigorous reading of weak signals. For foresight practitioners, the mission is to imagine what possible futures can be created and provide strategy a vision (or multiple visions) to facilitate a meaningful dialogue and a road map to close any competency gap between today and tomorrow.

"Don't despair: despair suggests you are in total control and know what is coming. You don't— surrender to events with hope."

— Alain de Botton

Strategic foresight is a deliberate and systematic process concerned with establishing well-informed future-oriented perspectives that help guide and inspire innovation, planning, and decision making. It helps us understand, anticipate, and prepare for change by equipping us with the tools and resources needed to ask provocative questions, challenge and test assumptions, rethink goals, and explore meaningful strategic alternatives. It encourages the deliberate and systematic exploration of uncertainties and their potential impact on behaviors and relationships.

WHY DOES BUSINESS NEED STRATEGIC FORESIGHT?

To help to prevent or prepare for surprises.
Within dynamic and discontinuous environments, foresight helps organizations better understand the variables influencing the pace, nature, and possible impacts of change. It addresses and confronts the need to continuously orient, reorient, plan, and act within volatile, complex, and uncertain business landscapes so that we're not caught off guard by change. Identifying and questioning the significance of the variables influencing and driving "change" ultimately help us anticipate and prepare for future conditions.

To help to establish and maintain competitive advantage.
Practicing foresight helps an organization gain a more robust understanding of how competitive dynamics might be changing and where gaps and opportunities might exist. This, in turn, helps enrich an organization's latent innovation potential, resources, and maneuverability. This is often accomplished by strengthening the ability to define and occupy opportunity spaces faster and with greater competence.

To positively influence and support innovation.

Foresight is one of many critical inputs or raw ingredients that help frame, fuel, and manage innovation. Any organization with an 18- to 36-month innovation cycle that is drawing on trend analysis to shape its future might as well throw in the towel. By the time you're ready to launch, your trends are old news. Foresight draws on trends— but it is not about trends today but rather what they might evolve into tomorrow. It can be used at the front end as a guide, as fuel, filter, or catalyst. And it can be used postinnovation as an amplifier or critical future proofing lens.

To empower and engage.

Practicing foresight helps individuals and organizations develop and improve their ability to identify future opportunities and transform them into meaningful outcomes. Developing and practicing these skills also builds the confidence necessary to make decisions within dynamic, uncertain, ambiguous, and less tangible contexts.

"Create your future from your future, not your past."

— Werner Erhard

WHAT ARE WEAK SIGNALS?

DESIGN THINKING AND STRATEGIC FORESIGHT

Design thinking is about solving "wicked" problems. As the speed of change continues to increase the complexity of doing business, new and more complex systems and even more "wicked" problems will continue to emerge. The race is on between bigger challenges and quicker solutions.

Foresight is an iterative and cumulative learning process that employs the design thinking tool kit, which includes environmental scanning, context mapping, archetype creation, and scenario development. It offers ways to explore, learn, and make sense of the variables and uncertainties shaping possible futures by questioning their relevance, illustrating their qualities and potential, and describing their influence on existing models and relationships.

Exploring the future and its uncertainties should be a daily activity sustained by individuals throughout the organization. Done properly, it should align more closely with planning, strategy, and innovation cycles.

To help organizations win that race there are many foresight tools, processes, and methods that can be employed, most of which begin with weak signals.

In the 1970s, Igor Ansoff, an applied mathematician, business manager, and the father of strategic management, noticed that failures in strategic management were causally linked to organizations overlooking vague, anomalous, ambiguous, yet critical information. To rectify that, he developed the weak signal theory.

For him, weak signals represented change or the potential for it. This change can, at first glance, be insignificant (such as the emergence of P2P file sharing) or highly disruptive (such as digital cameras). These signals are not facts or trends. Rather, as signs of new and emerging capabilities that could disrupt or transform existing norms, they represent subtle changes in reality that will manifest in individual or organizational behaviors, needs, desires, or values.

For example, early research investment in an obscure technical domain may be an obvious, strong signal of things to come for experts working within that context who may, even at the very early stages, understand the potential impact of the new capability. For those of us who are outsiders unfamiliar with this particular domain, that signal is still weak.

Beginning with weak signals, there are a number of component parts to the strategic foresight process, discussed next.

Business Challenge 03

Change

All companies must endure change to survive or grow. Our dynamic world continues to include unexpected events that cause disruption and uncertainty. The dirty little secret of change is that there is no theory for change. Change is the heart of leadership, and leaders must understand its context before designing and implementing any change program. They must anticipate everything possible to avoid and manage resistance to change. Rather than suppressing it, they must encourage an expression of concerns and critiques. Leaders also need to avoid people thinking that change is for change's sake.

Organizations need to plan for change. At a minimum, they should be able to effectively react to problems as they arise. At a maximum, they should know how to anticipate change and capitalize on opportunities that emerge from it. Simply stated, an organization that not only is prepared for but expects change is one that can overcome challenges.

As I mentioned at the beginning of this book, we are living in an age where change is reshaping industries and categories. Whether it's the bursting economic bubbles of the past decade, shifts in regulations, competition from emerging markets, new consumer expectations, or the impact of consumer conversations on the role, value, and legitimacy of brands, the business landscape today is very different from the one most current chief executive officers (CEOs) first entered.

The research and literature on change indicate that the number one reason for the success or failure of a change initiative hinges on the leadership skills, level of energy, and knowledge of the individuals responsible for leading the change. In light of this, one obvious question arises: What leadership behaviors or competencies are most strongly associated with effectively leading or overseeing change initiatives? You won't get a straight answer for this.

Work environments that nurture the ability to change and encourage employees to develop new and creative ideas will almost always outlast their competitors. Many companies cannot meet the challenges of change because it is easier to stay satisfied with current processes instead of working toward improvement. Striving for change and growth is what keeps companies competitive.

But most companies are designed and built for efficiency and predictability. Few are flexible enough or agile enough to handle the full scope of change as it exists in the real world. Wide-stemming cultural changes regarding how and why people use goods and services are not evaluated correctly through market research. Employees are not empowered to creatively frame solutions to endemic organizational problems. And most companies find it easier to deal with glitches in the system

as they arise, rather than be sensitive, intuitive, and creative in the development of preemptive change strategies. This creates a chain reaction of error. For many companies, this resistance to change is the beginning of a slow and continuous decline. Products become obsolete. Brands become irrelevant. Organizations become complacent.

Organizational change ultimately comes down to dealing with three components:

1/ **Discrepancy**
"We have a strong case for change."

2/ **Appropriateness**
"We have the right strategy and stakeholders are on board."

3/ **Efficacy**
"We can handle it and are committed and confident we will survive."

A company's agenda for change might be strategically sound and seemingly able to pave the way forward for years, but visions are susceptible to error and unforeseeable events. To help guard against the chaos of change, a company can use sense making as a means to remain strategically agile and nimble.

THINKING POINTS

You've seen all those photos of design thinkers or creative consultants surrounded by Post-it Notes and probably wondered what they were doing. In many cases, it's sense making. But sense making is about more than using Post-it Notes.

Sense making involves the process of creating mental models or mental maps that serve as memory representations with a salient visual imagery component expressed in terms of concepts, ideas, and knowledge. They are used to explain events, not isolated stimuli, which helps with connecting the dots and making decisions in complex and dynamic environments. Every organization needs to find visual, interactive, and "movable" ways to organize the raw inputs of sense making that, well, make sense to it. Don't get romanced by looking cool. Be effective: Define the best way for your organization to identify, organize, cluster, and prioritize the information on the wall.

Sense making is not a linear exercise, and it is not a process that turns information into insight. Sense making doesn't always have clear starting and ending points. *Visualization* is often used interchangeably with *sense making*, but visualization is not just a shared image with intent; it also implies the proactive use of shaping actions to reduce risk and uncertainty, probing actions to discover system effect implications or opportunities, and modeling actions that include behavioral and cognitive aspects to test and/or transform the environment. Visualization is central to sense making.

Business Challenge 04

Maintaining Relevance

All brands need to establish visibility, purpose, meaning, and credibility to be considered relevant in a category. Through innovation, an organization can elevate itself above its competitors and render them largely irrelevant to consumers. This is quite different from brand preference. Relevance is felt deeper and can create a clear divide between brands.

Innovating in a white space category or subcategory is imperative for market success today. In virtually all categories, from beverages to computers to financial services to air travel, marketing and product improvements rarely affect the sales or profits of a brand because of habitual consumer behavior. Meaningful changes in sales almost always relate to an offering that is created through substantial or transformational innovation.

The expectations of consumers are rising at the same time that many brands are becoming more resourceful and savvy at gaining attention and tailoring their unique selling propositions and reasons to believe to fit the market. But customers are becoming more demanding of companies to stay relevant to their ever-changing lifestyles. Relevance is extremely difficult to maintain long term. Over time, brands must rethink and redefine the value that they bring to consumers. It's getting tougher to lock in on value propositions that will truly satisfy. Value redefinition is a design approach that helps develop a new voice and meaning that will not only resonate with consumers but also sideswipe the competition.

Design Thinking Approach 04

Value Redefinition

Design thinking seeks relevance by promoting harmony with the identities, aspirations, attitudes, beliefs, needs, and desires that shape the ways people perceive and define value. It recognizes that individual perceptions and interpretations of value are constantly in flux and therefore aims to identify the underlying forces influencing this change. It aspires to develop greater empathy among people, brands, and business by observing, engaging with, and listening closely to people. To do this, the focus must be on establishing, framing, and stimulating the right conversations that will power up real insights that help businesses redefine value and maintain their relevance in the face of change.

The design thinking approach to redefining value begins with people, not products. It seeks to locate the functional, emotional, social, and cultural values that already exist within or can be designed into a brand's DNA and align those with the current and emerging values of consumers.

There are many ways to identify and interpret the shifting and relative nature of value. On the brand side of the equation, being honest and authentic is the best policy. Let's face it: Brand teams are so immersed in their daily challenges and their particular brand culture that they fail to see the forest for the trees.

"Price is what you pay. Value is what you get."

— Warren Buffett

Having oversubscribed to the mythology of their brand, few of them are ready, willing, and able to admit what they can't admit: The soda is not refreshing; the detergent is pumping toxins into the water; the mobile phone is clunky; the service sucks; it's not really about convenience; and you're nothing but a me-too innovation organization.

On the consumer side of the equation, rigorous and empathetic human-centric research is the best practice. It's simple really, and we'll get to it shortly: You will never truly understand how people define value of products and services through online surveys, consumer panels, and focus groups.

There is a complex and dynamic suite of factors that combine to influence our notion of value. We associate value with the satisfaction or fulfillment of a need. That is, value is associated with a product, service, system, artifact, or relationship that provides a means to a desired end. From another perspective, value is linked to actualization. Something is valuable when it serves a meaningful purpose and provides a benefit that equals or outweighs its cost.

This perception of value is shaped by factors such as personal experience, needs, wants, desires, and expectations. In addition, inherited social cultural norms and the sheer force of fitting in socially influence our notion of values. But many of these inherited norms are more fluid today than ever before, constantly being shaped and reshaped by new information, ideas, relationships, and opinions that challenge definitions of value.

In setting out to manage customer value, you may grapple first with the concept of how customers perceive value and how they are influenced by marketing or pre-conception or how technology or emerging behavior trends are shaping how value is defined and delivered. Customer value is at the core of any competitive strategy and is often least managed, often resulting in individual marketing, brand, product development, and pricing decisions being made rather than a conscious strategic and design exercise being undertaken.

Here's a starting point to clarify how customers perceive and define the value of your brand or business:

01/ Identify the functional, social, cultural, and historical reasons that have driven value for your brand, product, or business. How has it been meaningful before, and why? Now, compare that to today and identify the drivers and intensity of those changes.

02/ Determine how your key customers rate you versus competitors on these value drivers. Represent these value drivers through visual mapping to illustrate the differences between key segments.

03/ Define and articulate each of these value drivers in the context of the users.

04/ Identify the rate of change on each of these dimensions and look for signals to confirm which ones are slowing down and which ones are accelerating.

05/ Conduct a workshop to identify opportunities to redefine value ahead of the game on those dimensions that have the largest gap between how they are being served and what their needs are.

06/ Design and conduct a participative design session in which you invite customers to talk about these dimensions to validate your assumptions and allow them to co-create new value combinations.

07/ Analyze the results and conduct a value-mapping workshop to explore how to redefine value to change the competitive landscape. The success of Ikea, Netflix, Zipcar, Nintendo, Amazon.com, Salesforce .com, Zappos, and EasyJet are all classic examples of companies that have been successful in redefining customer value to change the game.

THINKING POINTS

What is our current understanding of customer value? Have the top three attributes valued by customers been validated recently? Which of them are still relevant, and which ones are definitely not? Consider the following nonexhaustive attributes when thinking about customer value.

· **How can you solve my problem quickly?** Value is based on the simplest, cheapest, and most effective ways to solve a customer problem or complete a job. Focus on those three that will help you to secure a strong position.

· **How can you solve my problem the way I want it?** Value is based on a high degree of personalized preferences and is not a one-solution-fits-all scenario.

· Focus on customization and helping customers see that their problem and your solution are somewhat unique and that you are ready to tackle any kind of problem within a certain domain.

· **How can you solve my problem anytime, anyplace?** Value here is defined by your high degree of readiness and accessibility, and even the customer is expecting to pay for the extra cost. Focus on the service, reliability, and experience and define your market based on how availability is important for those segments.

· **How can you solve a problem for me that I don't want to know about?** Value here is defined by how you can eliminate some of your customer's problems with as little involvement as possible from the customer. Focus on how you can help them handle those parts of the tasks that most people would rather not have to deal with or even hear about.

· **How can you solve a problem that I don't even know I have?** Value here is driven by your supreme leadership in any domain. Your customer will believe whatever you communicate and will trust that you are thinking ahead and can anticipate problems throughout a job.

Business Challenge 05

Extreme Competition

So much shareholder value has been destroyed in the past 10 years as a result of mismanagement, poor strategic decision making, and an inability to react to disruptive innovation or extreme competition. Traditional competitive strategy often leads to further commoditization. Look at almost any industry, and you will find companies struggling to differentiate what they have to offer from everything else in the marketplace. Differentiation needs to be relevant and meaningful, so it's hardly surprising that one of the most common complaints from senior executives is: "My product is becoming commoditized, and the pace of commoditization is accelerating. What should I do?"

If business decisions and their tactical approaches were made through purely logical and analytical means, our world would look very different. We would arrive at solutions optimized for efficiency. Competition would be reduced down to highly predictable shifts. And consumers would see all the world's products and services as interchangeable commodities.

But competition in business is not shaped by objectivity. It's shaped by creativity and innovation that accelerates change and drives differentiation. This makes conducting business less like tic-tac-toe and more like chess, where, despite the availability of known moves and patterns of behaviors, the best business leaders deviate from the most common paths and take new avenues toward victory.

Today, navigating those paths is more challenging than ever, thanks, in large part, to overcommoditization. Although some products and brands stand apart from the crowd because of key factors such as craftsmanship, quality, heritage, and long-standing semiotics of value, the majority of products and brands out there are suffering—or unknowingly preparing to suffer—from a lack of differentiation.

When all you have is another hotel brand, energy drink, luxury purse, smartphone, or hybrid car, what do you do? The answer might be experience design. Innovating through experience design offers companies a high degree of differentiation in some of the most ubiquitous product and service categories.

Design Thinking Approach 05

Experience Design

Experience design is a holistic and multidisciplinary approach to creating meaningful contexts of interaction and exchange among users and products, services, systems, and spaces. It considers the sensation of interactions with a product or service on physical and cognitive levels. The boundaries of an experience can be expansive and include the sensorial, symbolic, temporal, and spatial. It can include tangible customer value as well as emotional value. It's not just about interface, usability, or customer service flow. It's about the word: *experience*.

Experience design is an established set of design thinking practices that, when performed properly, can enchant customers and create a sense of loyalty that will keep them keep coming back to you every time. By maximizing each and every dimension of an experience at every stage in, for example, a shopping experience—discovery, interaction, departure, and postdeparture—it considers how customers engage with a product, service, or brand in order to set the stage for something truly different, special, and even magical.

"Focus on the journey, not the destination. Joy is found not in finishing an activity but in doing it."

– Greg Anderson

To set this stage, organizations must consider and evaluate not only how a product or service functions but also how it communicates meaning and intent. Experience design highlights the importance of developing a clear understanding of consumer needs, cultures, expectations, assumptions, and capacities. How an experience speaks to consumers will ultimately determine how one product or service feels different from another.

Design thinkers critically observe and evaluate the various experiences they encounter throughout their day and reflect on how one may differ from another by asking, What makes a better experience, and why? In fact, most of us do this on some level every day, especially those of us who share our experiences with others in a highly opinionated, social media–driven world.

With increasing competition across multiple categories, the distance between one brand's price, features, and design and another's is becoming shorter and shorter. Intuitively, however, most of us know the difference between Tom's Shoes and Converse, United and Southwest, Target and Walmart, Taco Bell and Chipotle, and Dodge and Mercedes-Benz because we have experienced one or both.

Design thinking seeks to explore the wiggle room between brands like these and transform it into a competitive chasm. When that difference is or might be emotional, design thinkers ask: When does the value of a product exceed its functional value? At what point does emotive value reach a point of diminishing return? What is the value of the emotive premium? Should there be an emotive premium at all? Can we engineer emotive elements into the design without adding cost?

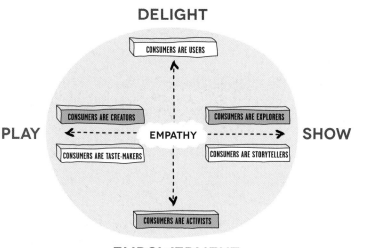

DELIGHT

CONSUMERS ARE USERS

CONSUMERS ARE CREATORS

CONSUMERS ARE EXPLORERS

PLAY EMPATHY **SHOW**

CONSUMERS ARE TASTE-MAKERS

CONSUMERS ARE STORYTELLERS

CONSUMERS ARE ACTIVISTS

EMPOWERMENT

The answers to these questions lie buried in the nature of experience. All experiences are functional, social, cultural, and personal. They are important, relevant, and meaningful to people. They have a past, present, and even a future subject to reflection and reflexivity. To communicate and reinforce a value proposition, they need to be thoughtfully facilitated through the purposeful design of brands, products, services, interfaces, and interactions.

How?

Social experiences. Social is about more than Facebook and Pinterest, okay? How can you make your brand more social? Can you connect people? Can you help forge meaningful relationships? Could your stores be redesigned to transform them into more social spaces?

Learning experiences. Can your brand, your stores, or your online property shape learning and mastery, where your customers have access to experiences that make them smarter, faster, stronger, or better?

Meaningful experiences. Beyond social and learning, how else can you give your customers the opportunity to experience greater meaning in their lives through your brand? If your first instinct is to jump to cause marketing, think again. You need to do more than increase impressions by giving away money.

Geeky experiences. Who doesn't love to geek out on what they love? In the design of stores, for example, consider the immediate expression of experience that walking into an All Saints store with their sewing machines in the window does for apparel geeks or the huge digital displays at Burberry do for fashion fanatics who want to feel the runway.

UNDERSTANDING THE FOUR KEY DIMENSIONS OF EXPERIENCE DESIGN

Because human experience is multidimensional so, too, is the design thinking approach to it. Here are four ways to get started:

1/ Determine the scope of the experience.
Decide on a starting point and an end point. You can expand boundaries, but you need to have them at the beginning. With scope comes the breadth of interactions in store, marketing, digital, and beyond. Where and why do you want to or need to engage customers?

2/ Understand the intensity of experience.
Some experiences are simply a routine way to get something done quickly and effortlessly. Some are complex, intense, and highly emotive. You need to analyze and prioritize your effort based on those parts of the experience that are both highly rational and emotive. That's where the intensity is high, as well as the stakes.

3/ Identify the key experience triggers.
Experiences are triggered by stimuli that elicit recognition. These could include visuals, symbols, photographs, videos, smells, and sound. Experience designers need to consider what combinations of these are the triggers for brand recognition and how to use them to support delivery.

4/ Deepen the customer's engagement to evoke meanings.
Experience design achieves the highest impact when it evokes meanings. Sometimes these are distant from the product or service, but when executed authentically (meaning it's a part of your business culture), they become very close to the brand. At the center of meanings are core values. If you can express them well, customers will subscribe to them.

THINKING POINTS

You may not have a customer experience strategy, but you have a customer experience regardless of whether you create it consciously. Every company provides a customer experience. You may not have total control over that experience, but there are always opportunities to make it emotive and memorable and to make it work for you. So how can you design an emotional experience? The implicit problem is knowing what will work or not work in terms of emotional engagement and economic and operational feasibility. It begins with using customer journey mapping to visually illustrate an individual customer's needs and goals, the series of interactions and information necessary to fulfill those needs, and the resulting emotional states a customer experiences throughout the entire process.

Customer journey mapping succeeds when these exercises are based on ethnographic research and contextual inquiry that allow researchers to experience and perceive the emotions of customers, thereby making it possible for managers to convey more than just anecdotal quotations. The outcome of the exercise shows how customers feel throughout their journey, and customer journey maps invite stakeholders to enter the world of customers and share in their experience. In turn, stakeholders are better able to convey their story to management and frontline employees. This should be the starting point for your experience design.

Business Challenge 06

Standardization

Standardization is a necessary cost driver for every company. It is a means to achieve operational, cost, and performance efficiencies by streamlining activities, leveraging technologies, and maintaining employee workflow to reduce operating costs. But standardizing practices can mean losing the personal touch, reducing the choices customers have, and disconnecting employees. This is the balancing act every company must master: How do you stay lean, mean, and efficient while maintaining the human qualities that will ultimately endear you to people?

To streamline operations and be as profitably productive as possible, every company seeks to better leverage the powers of enterprise technology, design rule-driven workflows, and automate repetitive tasks. It makes sense not to reinvent the wheel every time you need to go for a drive. Regardless of the reasons for pursuing it, however, the race for standardization can come at a serious and often unforeseen expense.

Like companies, many people prefer efficiency to inefficiency. We like reliability. We like consistency. And we like to do things well and quickly. But we also like a degree of feeling in what we do. When a company's primary focus is on making standardization its priority, it can lose sight of the emotional quotient of its brand and alienate consumers. Here, for example, a standardization of market research practices can fail to see real

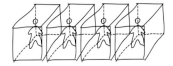

human needs, a standardization of product design practices can get sucked into looking no further than today's coolest feature, a standardization of segmentation can miss valuable opportunities to serve the underserved, and an internal mandate for standardization can take some stakeholders' eyes off the real prize of today: a customer-centric culture.

Contrary to what some design-minded authors will tell you, this critique of standardization is not based on a belief that companies that value sameness will be less successful in innovation than companies that value difference. Like people, companies are complex creatures, each with its own history, qualities, and characteristics that, when it comes to innovation, cannot be reduced down to the kind of Top Ten Ways list that proliferates at the lead of your LinkedIn page. Standardization can make internal processes more efficient and effective. It can clearly establish common goals of performance that every employee must meet. It can provide common platforms that make a supply chain run faster and cheaper. And it can be a rallying cry for product departments to make life simpler and more pleasant for consumers through the simplicity of design. Or it can't.

One of the most common challenges that clients in industries from consumer packaged goods to technology raise with my teams when we are scoping out a project is that no matter how great an insight or idea might be, it will ultimately be subjected to company standards. In some cases, the standardization of legacy manufacturing poses a big challenge to innovation.

How do you maintain operational efficiencies without sacrificing innovation opportunities and the human lens through which they will ultimately be identified?

Although every good consulting firm worth its billable hours understands that it's going to be a very long, uphill battle to get a company that sells circles to consider squares, clients—particularly in the world of packaged food—are often quick to point out how their company's innovation capabilities are restricted by factors such as size, shape, and ingredients. We all know why the machines were made the way they were made 20 or 30 years ago—efficiency—but that shouldn't stop us from considering a day where squares sell more than circles because consumers need or want them. Here, the standardization of the past can restrict the opportunities of the future.

In other cases, we deploy anthropologists to perform contextual inquiries and they use the simplest, most concise, and most engaging language to communicate the value of an insight that they believe could be leveraged to create real competitive differentiation for a client. But when the client's market research department has such a fixed and highly rigid way of approaching, thinking about, and talking about customers and how it identifies their so-called needs using words such as *target, segment, actionable*, and the worst ever, *reason to believe*, standardization becomes the enemy of innovation. It restricts vision. It dampens empathy. And it ultimately causes companies to miss out on potentially transformative opportunities.

The balancing act of standardization is a difficult one: How do you maintain operational efficiencies without sacrificing innovation opportunities and the human lens through which they will ultimately be identified?

Design Thinking Approach 06

Humanization

Great design refutes standardization in favor of the gentler, more human, and more emotional aspects of customer experience. It's the joy, pathos, laughter, and anxiety found in each can of soda, user interface, and public transit terminal that customers might not be able to openly describe but nonetheless deeply feel. Design thinkers are sensitive to the human touch points that encourage and foster such emotions as profound moments of attachment to a product, service, or brand.

The lack of humanization in experiences is not always purposeful but rather naturally occurs as standardization takes hold. A physician who treats scores of injured patients during an emergency must detach from emotion in order to give everyone what they need. Similarly, products, services, and business models naturally detach from the softer side of life to operate efficiently. But ultimately, customers don't care about the operations behind their favorite coffee brand; they care about the exhilaration they feel when they have a cup of coffee in their hands.

Design thinkers remind businesses that they are ultimately responding to human values, beliefs, and needs. They understand that efficiency and standardization will always have a place in business processes but recognize that it's the human touch points that resonate most in real-life customer experience to give products, services, and brands true value and meaning.

HUMANIZATION FROM AND WITHIN CULTURE

Great design is only as good as its ability to connect and forge relationships with the people who ultimately use it. This means that the first task of great design is to understand the cultural touch points to humanization that make such relationships possible.

Culture is the shared values, beliefs, and performances that define a group of people and their behaviors. Without a thorough understanding of culture, businesses cannot understand the human emotions that either make or break customer experiences. As a valuable tool in design thinking, culture is a springboard for unpacking opportunities for humanization in design.

Understanding culture means unpacking all the social meanings (and emotions) that define a particular customer's experience. For example, drinking coffee can involve the emotions associated with enjoying that wistful first cup on a foggy Saturday morning, recovering from a college all-night study party, or kicking back for an after-dinner "release" after overindulging at a favorite restaurant. It is a unit of cultural capital for the barista, the coffee connoisseur, and the housewife who wants her special treat when the kids take their nap. So many emotions and contexts define the coffee experience. Design thinkers unpack each coffee context in search of humanization opportunities. From this, a more holistic picture of drinking coffee in the real world emerges—defining what coffee means to consumers in their everyday lives. More culturally relevant designs ensue, providing brands meaningful customer interactions that stand the test of time.

Humanization doesn't just come from culture; it is also produced from within cultures. Designers, like the businesses they work for, are people who impart social values and beliefs on the things they produce. Design thinkers seek to understand the cultures not only of others but also of themselves, recognizing that their own emotions, practices, and belief systems inform what, how, and why they do what they do. To balance this, design thinkers encourage a dialogue between everyone in the product or service ecosystem by consulting with the company, their partners, brand representatives, and end customers.

"The essence of being
human is that one does
not seek perfection."

—George Orwell

Failure is the only opportunity to begin more intelligently.

HUMANIZING THROUGH LANGUAGE

Consider the language that most businesspeople use today: *target, driving performance, leveraging outcomes, actionable*, and other taglines that make managers feel like they're in some kind of special ops group. Here, the language of power, pragmatism, and predictability creates the illusion that businesses are machines. They're not. Businesses are organizational cultures filled with human beings who define and attach value to what they do every day. And, oh yeah, they are also organizational cultures that should be fulfilling human needs.

If all businesses are human enterprises that produce things made for human beings, it's time to start humanizing the business narrative. Design thinking seeks to reinsert human-centered qualities that can introduce new meaning. This means using real talk about the personal histories, dreams, and desires that define each worker, team, business unit, and office to produce human narratives of company culture that resonate worldwide. Remember: Each worker isn't a cog in the wheel. The suit that goes to work also goes home. It's worn by a person with a meaningful life—and that's a valuable brand story of not just what a company does but who a company is: its people.

THINKING POINTS

One route to greater humanization is reassessing how your organization does research on consumers and talks about or represents them. On the research front, consider hiring people who are specialists in human culture: sociologists, anthropologists, and other social scientists who specialize in understanding us without putting us in focus group facilities and looking at tracking studies. On the talking and representation front, remember that language structures all cultures; organizations that talk about *targets* and *segments* distance themselves from people with every utterance.

Humanization can be leveraged by usability, human factors, customer experience design, and brand storytelling. All customers, employees, and their friends are part of your story network and can all be part of your humanization design; if you let them bring their humanity to your brand or organization, they'll also bring your brand into their networks and their lives. Brands that have been humanized attract and sustain communities of real live people and make customers more forgiving when organizations make mistakes.

Business Challenge 07

Creative Culture

Big or small, many companies fall into the trap of trying to innovate the "right" way. By spending so much time, energy, and resources on getting it right and avoiding failure, not enough time, energy, and resources are dedicated to playful, experimental creation.

Innovative cultures are creative cultures. Few of us would disagree that those companies that innovate well have some degree of creativity in their DNA. But having a creative culture is not about a workplace that's filled with funky chairs, table tennis games, a video game zone, or Post-it Notes. It's about recognizing, even celebrating, uncertainty and ambiguity from the get-go and applying your passion and skills—whether they live in the right or left side of the brain—to come up with ideas, find solutions, and solve problems in new and strategic ways.

Creativity cannot be taught. Some companies run occasional creative workshops with designers; hold creative events featuring artists, architects, or chefs; and encourage creative projects on company time hoping this will promote it among employees so that they come up with more innovative solutions in their daily work. Others companies, such as Pixar, whose Pixar University runs more than 100 courses on everything from improv to cooking to self-defense, nurture the creativity of employees as an ongoing, in-house initiative that supports a macro organizational attitude. For those who do it well, however, the creative capital of teams and companies is earned only through experiences of trial, error, and occasional failure. Here, the name of the game is experimentation, and when done well, it nourishes a culture of curiosity and excitement.

Because most companies are run by the numbers and tend to be very risk-averse, the attitude toward creativity in those whose bottom line is not connected to a creative output (such as animation) tends to be very narrow when it comes to the softer, fuzzier, warmer side of innovation. In fact, many such companies are actually fearful of creativity, thinking it's a plague against efficiency. They're wrong.

If an organization's culture is not engineered or nurtured to truly be innovative and to take risks, it will surely fall victim to competitors that are more tolerant of or driven by creative experimentation. In a business age fueled by how well new ideas do in the face of intense competition and overstandardization, creativity and design thinking need to be the centerpiece of any company.

In 1995's *Defying the Crowd: Cultivating Creativity in a Culture of Conformity*, American psychologists Robert Sternberg and Todd Lubart argue that "People are not born creative; rather, creativity can be developed." Putting forward their investment theory of creativity, which describes an influence of the environment on the judgment of creativity, they suggest that the relationship between people and the environment is like that between investors and a stock market. Here, creative people are like good investors who buy low and sell high. Innovative ideas might not be considered by the market to be creative at first, but these people try their best to change that judgment in order to sell high. Once the market has been convinced of the creative value of the idea or product, these people move on to the next idea that will, not surprisingly, be unappreciated at first. Why are these people so creative and so tenacious? According to Sternberg and Lubart, they are able to draw on six resources that are critical to cultivating creativity: intelligence, knowledge, thinking styles, personality, motivation, and the environment.

These are the raw ingredients for building a creative culture. Design thinking offers many ways to help a company develop such a culture, but the one that stands out the most—that encourages trial, error, experimentation, and creative play—is rapid prototyping.

Design Thinking Approach 07

Rapid Prototyping

Rapid prototyping is an iterative learning process that acquires and expresses increasingly complex information of higher fidelity over time through repetitive and cumulative cycles of build, test, see, and refine. Prototypes are traditionally used in design and engineering environments, but when they become integral to other organizational cultures, they serve to develop a creative mind-set that is able to effectively focus on imagining, socializing, and testing any idea, including work processes, team structures, business models, and, of course, products and services. Because every output of design thinking begins as a prototype, think of them as part of a culture and not specifically as a tool.

Most businesspeople are familiar with the "fail fast, fail cheap, and fail early" concept. Design thinking suggests another dimension to this rule: "Learn fast, learn cheap, and learn early." Prototyping is the way to open up that dimension; it's a relatively low-cost, hands-on activity that helps bring people on to the same conceptual page, uncover new knowledge, and identify and mitigate design and development risks early on. This is done to avoid downstream costs while also building up critical assets for the internal and external communication and socialization of ideas. As part of the hands-on approach, prototyping typically seeks to involve and engage multiple stakeholders and so-called end users as participants at every stage of iteration, from paper to final production.

Prototyping is a currency for creative dialogue. It embraces play behaviors as a critical component of imagination and ideation. By creating multiple feedback loops through employee-to-employee iterations and employee-to-user testing and refinement of illustrations, models, or product and service mock-ups, it is a way to produce new knowledge and make ambiguous concepts more tangible. The concept is quite simple: It's much easier for people to articulate what they want by playing with prototypes than by enumerating business requirements in Excel or PowerPoint. Given that almost every organization claims it wants to design a more agile process for faster product development, it's shocking how few of them utilize rapid prototyping as a way to accelerate learning and speed up feedback loops that can assess potential implications and generate shared mental models of the business problem.

"You may never know what results come of your action, but if you do nothing there will be no result."

— Mahatma Gandhi

THE BENEFITS OF PROTOTYPING IN BUSINESS DESIGN

01/ Increase team ownership.
Rapid prototypes can ensure that all those leading or affected by changes to a company are involved in understanding and perhaps even shaping the future in a context that comes to life in a more tangible way.

02/ See the possibilities.
Rapid prototypes expose potential solutions, obstacles, and unanticipated outcomes of an idea. By bringing everyone on to the same page to discuss and develop solutions, they create a shared understanding of a current vision or a future state.

03/ Deepen insight.
Rapid prototypes let you see the big picture without losing sight of the details. By utilizing them in context with both stakeholders and potential users, teams are able to better identify the kind of usability issues, workarounds, gaps, brand connections, and opportunity extensions that drive development and refinement.

04/ Promote cross-functional collaboration.
Prototyping facilitates social bonds among employees who may not have the chance to interact and empathize with one another. The experiences, artifacts, and stories that emerge from prototyping become a part of that group's shared narrative, which can be passed down and transmitted to others within the organization. In addition, the bonds that form among employees engaged in co-creative activities increase relationships by reducing assumptions, stigmas, and other barriers to communication.

05/ Improve visibility and predictability.
Rapid prototypes provide a blueprint for change that can be as detailed as needed, leading to a clear future state with concrete milestones and transparent progress. Whether it's about designing a product, a service, or a new way to work within a company, this results in increased predictability.

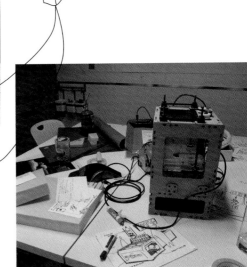

BUILDING, FOSTERING, AND EMBEDDING CREATIVE CONFIDENCE

Prototyping plays an important role in developing a more engaged and creative organizational culture by encouraging people to bring their ideas to life in a more tangible way. This makes it easier to share ideas with others and to leverage feedback to make improvements upon them. Encouraging and enabling aspects of prototyping across an organization can help foster a more creative culture that is more comfortable, confident, and capable in its ability to propose, explore, and learn about innovative solutions to problems and opportunities.

It is important for leaders to support a culture of prototyping with the right resources for creating, for example, dirty spaces—workshops or labs for making stuff with simple tools and basic materials such as paper, markers, foam, clay, cardboard, tape, and even computer-aided design (CAD) software or 3-D printers. There's no need to invest a lot of money; just demonstrate a commitment to prototyping and a willingness to encourage and support it in a tangible way. In addition, training sessions that introduce specific techniques and processes can be adopted to help improve existing skill sets and the quality of the prototypes.

💡 **THINKING POINTS**

Remember the excitement of show-and-tell when you were a kid? Or the thrill of story time? Prototyping can bring that magic back and facilitate the kind of dialogue and learning among employees that is sometimes lost. By promoting prototyping events where employees can showcase and share their work and ideas, companies will learn to work better and move faster to take advantage of new and disruptive opportunities.

Everyone can participate in rapid prototyping. You don't need to be creative. You need to be willing to try—sketch, draw, cartoon, map, make, and show. However rough and raw the prototype might be, every employee can get an idea down on paper to share and develop an idea.

by Harvard Business School professor Michael Porter in the 1980s. It's about lining up all of your business operations behind a central logic of value creation, and it is the most rigorous and practical strategy concept ever developed. The fit and differentiation concepts are also unlike business model design or business model innovation, which operate fuzzily around crafting value propositions, business activities, and a revenue model.

Business strategy and business model innovation diverge when we are dealing with radical business model innovation. Strategy is competing within today's defined market space and industry boundaries and perfecting a set of business activities that differentiate you from your competitors. Business model design is part of strategy innovation and is essentially about designing business activities around tomorrow's opportunities. Its main mission is to answer the following questions.

BUSINESS MODEL VERSUS BUSINESS STRATEGY

It is generally acceptable to use the terms *business strategy* and *business model* interchangeably, as long as we understand the subtle distinctions. Both are used to refer to all the components and activities that guide managerial decisions. There are four key distinctions between the two:

01/ Both describe the business system and activities that show how each of the pieces of a business fit together. However, strategy mainly deals with competition and sustaining differentiation, whereas business models focus on the interplay of different elements, relationships, and how value is being created, captured, and transferred. In short, the core focus is how you make money.

02/ Business strategy includes the organizational capabilities that have a direct impact on operational decisions and the organizational culture or on how a strategy is to be executed. A business model is more about how a business functions in the value chain or networks. Business model execution and resource allocation decisions are mostly neglected.

03/ A business model has a narrow focus on how a company can make money by focusing on pricing strategy, strategic partnerships, and channel choice. All of these decisions affect the top line and have as their goal the optimization of revenue or sometimes the survival of an early phase of a business. On the other hand, business strategy deals with much broader and deeper issues, including capital structure, cost structure, and asset utilization.

04/ Business models are subject to changes in technology and competitive dynamics and are therefore constantly subject to change themselves. On the other hand, once a strategy is set, it's all about the execution.

BUSINESS MODEL DESIGN FRAMEWORK

Forget what your company knows it can already do. Instead, begin this process by asking what value is being created today and how it aligns with established or emerging customer needs. What is the exchange of value between everyone in the ecosystem? How does the current system answer customer needs and create customer surplus while generating profit? This purposeful linking of interdependent activities performed by the company in collaboration with suppliers, partners, and customers is the essence of business model design.

A business model design exercise that puts the essential building blocks and their relationships in the value chain together makes it easier for managers to make decisions based on a better understanding of value flow and how a company makes money. They can adapt and fine-tune the business model once it is working. Explicating, capturing, and visualizing a business model will improve planning and provide a common understanding among key stakeholders. From a design thinking perspective, business model innovation leans toward exploring new approaches to the softer and less tangible qualities such as value proposition, organizational culture, values, and core competencies. Rather than building fixed assets or long-term infrastructure, there are mountains of opportunities to be discovered through more resourceful

and creative tactics. Design thinking approaches to business model innovation may examine and seek to exploit the latent and potential value existing within an organization by identifying how its core competencies, resources, and assets (including intellectual property) can be leveraged in new and innovative ways. Design thinking may seek to interpret the qualities and characteristics of this latent potential, question what part of the value chain an existing model sits within, and explore ways in which the organization's latent potential or untapped assets and resources can be realigned into a new model.

There has been little knowledge or practice development to date devoted to this important undertaking. It is as much a creative exercise as an analysis exercise. Here we provide a conceptual tool kit that enables readers to design their future business models and that also helps managers analyze and rethink their current designs so that they can be fine-tuned for the future. It needs to begin with identification of emerging behavior that will affect how value is being created today and identification of what the drivers of chance are. What is the value exchange among key parties involved, including everyone in the activity system such as the purchasers and consumers, which sometimes are different parties? How does the current system respond to customers' needs and create customer surplus while generating a profit for the company?

That objective is reflected in the customer value proposition that is linked to an economic logic that requires a host of activities that include the engagement of human, physical, and/or capital resources of any party to the business model to serve a specific purpose toward the fulfillment of the overall objective.

The purposeful design of interdependent activities performed by the company itself or in collaboration with suppliers, partners, and/or customers—is the essence of the business model design. It is basically a design thinking undertaking; experimenting and mapping links between different activities will provide insights into the processes that will enable the evolution or radical redesign of a company's activity system as its competitive environment changes or the business opportunity justifies it. The purposeful design through visual modeling and activities mapping within and across firm boundaries is the context of the business model design.

The company's revenue model plays an important role in the overall business model design. It is linked to a pricing strategy for specific products or services. The revenue model complements a business model design, and the two cannot be separated, just as a pricing strategy complements a marketing strategy. They are closely linked but yet distinctive. A business model is geared toward total value creation for all parties involved. It lays the foundations for the focal company's value capture by codifying the overall size of the pie, or the total value created in transactions, which can be considered the upper limit of the firm's value capture potential.

The business model design determines the company's bargaining power based on its strategic assets, access, and capabilities, as well as the intensity of the competition: The greater the total value created and the greater the focal firm's bargaining power, the greater the amount of value that the focal company can appropriate. How much of the total value the firm actually captures, however, depends on its revenue model and if there is any lock-in mechanism for the business model, such as barriers to switch. Business model design for an innovative product or service could have very different implications; it may not be about increasing the share or the size of the pie but about creating a new pie that has not existed previously but that can be scaled very quickly. The adoption curve of that new business can impact the business model as the business scales.

When designing a new business model, one precondition is to re examine assumptions regarding what to consider core capabilities to the company and the business boundaries. Strategic discussions including Who are we? What is unique about us? What businesses are we in? How do we differentiate? How do we create and capture value? and What is our operating model? Many value chain activities are

based on transactions only, and when design thinking is applied in business model design, we need to be creative and look at what existing and new activities should be considered for higher value. High value activities are the activities that either generate revenue directly or indirectly enable you to generate revenue. Unfortunately, many of the activities that companies perform are not high value but taking the same level of energy and resources to maintain operations.

STARTING WITH THE CONCEPT METAPHOR

To use design thinking for business model innovation, we need to start with the right conceptual metaphors to aid in the exploration of an organization's latent potential in relation to new and innovative business models. In the traditional world of business education this exercise would start from the value chain and apply the concept of fit to decide in what part of the value chain the company should choose to participate. But in design thinking, we start from the emerging customer needs and use that to map customer value clusters. Based on those cluster scenarios, we examine what value systems are not being fulfilled today. Each of those then provides relevant differentiation and sustaining market power. With that ideal state in mind, we can look at how existing capabilities can deliver against those activities.

In the process of designing the value delivery system, businesses also need to seek to identify which role—or position in the chain they currently occupy or would like to occupy—can potentially be eliminated or outsourced to a vendor to lessen capital investment, especially in times of scarce resources. This can often reduce organizational burdens while simultaneously opening paths toward innovation.

APPLIED DESIGN THINKING FOR BUSINESS MODEL DESIGN

This is where you can apply real design thinking to real subjects. Get your pencils out and your thinking caps on.

WHAT YOU'RE HEARING

UNDERNEATH THE SURFACE

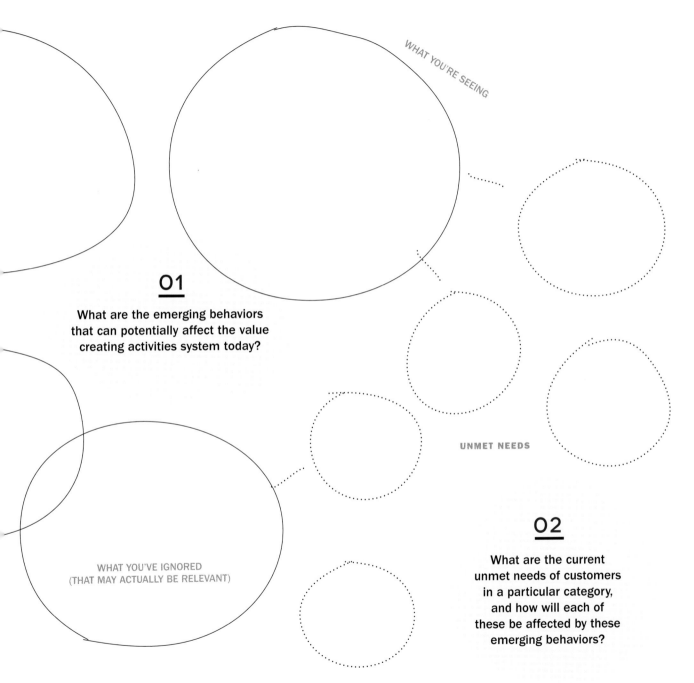

WHAT YOU'RE SEEING

01

What are the emerging behaviors that can potentially affect the value creating activities system today?

UNMET NEEDS

WHAT YOU'VE IGNORED
(THAT MAY ACTUALLY BE RELEVANT)

02

What are the current unmet needs of customers in a particular category, and how will each of these be affected by these emerging behaviors?

<u>03</u>

**How does each segment define value,
and are those definitions aligned with
what the company thinks?**

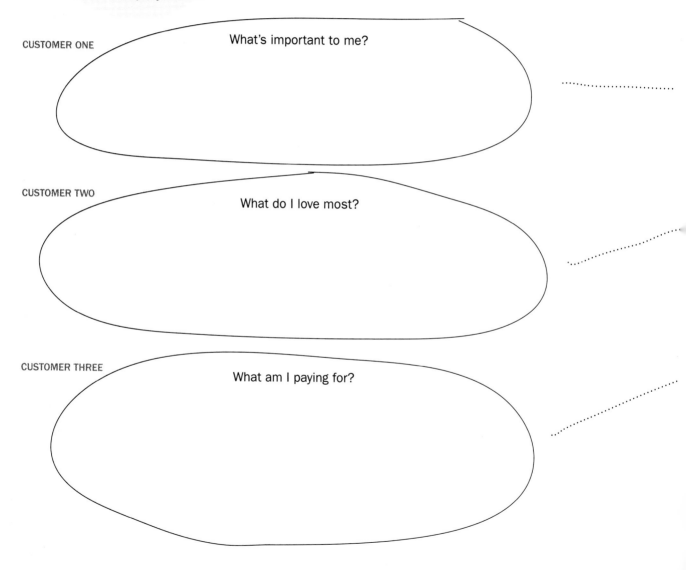

CUSTOMER ONE

What's important to me?

CUSTOMER TWO

What do I love most?

CUSTOMER THREE

What am I paying for?

**Using these definitions,
what assumptions do we make?**

**Identify the key gaps
and explore the reasons
behind what's causing the
differences.**

....

....

....

....

....

....

....

....

....

....

....

05

How is value being created and distributed in the current state?

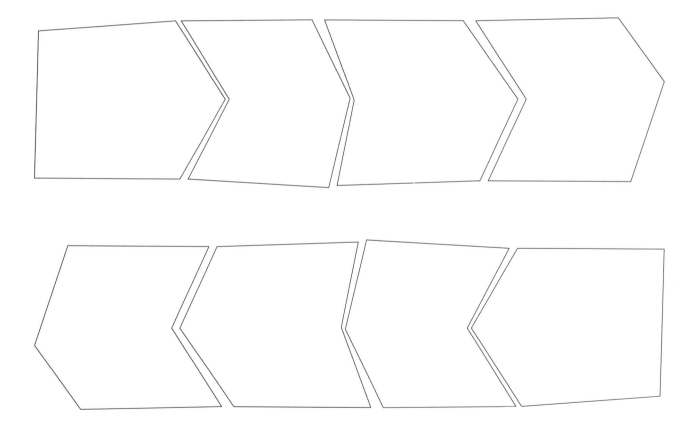

06

Is the business model based around a single stream of revenue or multiple streams? What is the logic behind these decisions?

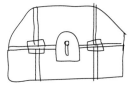

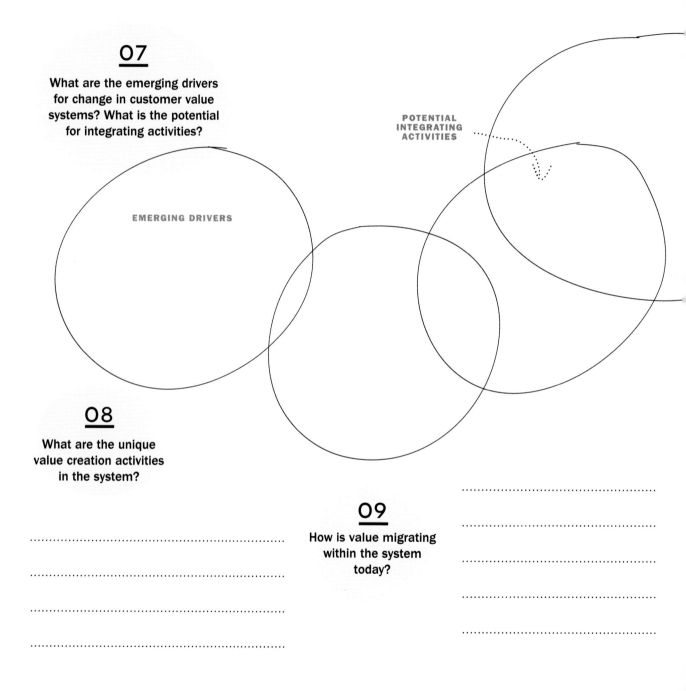

07

What are the emerging drivers for change in customer value systems? What is the potential for integrating activities?

POTENTIAL INTEGRATING ACTIVITIES

EMERGING DRIVERS

08

What are the unique value creation activities in the system?

09

How is value migrating within the system today?

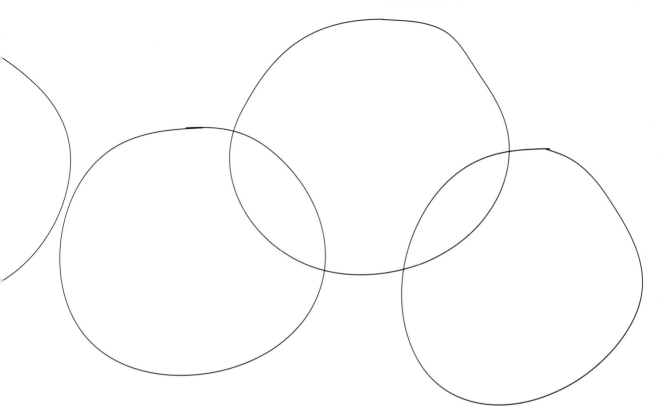

<u>10</u>

How do they all fit together to form the most attractive business system?

....

....

....

....

....

11

How does this value
creation and delivery system
compare to the current one?

12

Outline the distinctive
benefits of the old and the
new business models.

<u>13</u>

How would those benefits change over the short and medium term, and what causes the change?

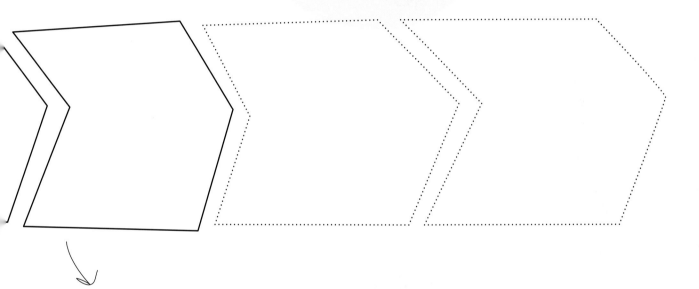

14

What are the other creative ways to combine capabilities and assets to deliver to these value systems?

15

What are the underlying revenue model options (for example, selling, licensing, subscriptions, advertising, sponsorship, transaction)?

....

....

....

....

....

....

....

....

....

....

16

**What are the other payer options?
Can this product be subsidized?
Are there bundling opportunities?**

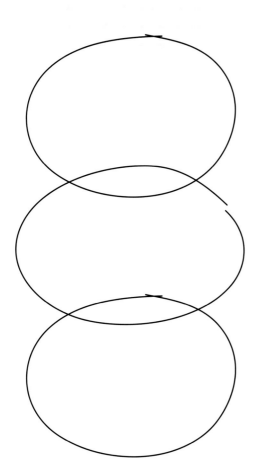

17

**What are the underlying purchase
behaviors affecting the revenue
model decision?**

18

**Does our revenue
model link to our
customers' value or
their success?**

3RD PARTY

19

**Does the business model
rely heavily on third-party
partnership to develop and
provide a revenue stream?**

20

At what point we need to explore changing a business model because of a change in revenue source?

....

....

....

....

....

....

21

How will the value migration evolve over the next three to five years? What is the estimated life span of this business model, and at what point does the current business model become invalid?

3 years   4 years   5 years

THINKING POINTS

The most sustainable competitive advantage lies in a robust business model design. Although on a surface level there are only limited business model options, companies competing using different business models can have very different outcomes. Analysis of business models cannot be mechanical and needs to be considered on a systems level, which often becomes complex. Network effects are an exogenous feature of technologies, and a winner-take-all end result is common among platform-based competition. Design thinking can be applied to visualize and identify the relationships and long term implications of different business models and their strengths and weaknesses. When they are performed as a simple spreadsheet exercise there is a false sense of certainty about the future. Spreadsheets won't provide users the ability to see the entire supply and demand relationship and it is the reason why so many new business models fail, even though they look robust on spreadsheets and in PowerPoint.

A business model redesign often requires transforming organizational structures, processes, and culture in addition to capabilities. This is often a missing consideration or an afterthought, a common cause of less successful business model design implementation. There is a strong link between business models and organizational form and decision-making structure. Most unique business models require the support of a unique organizational design.

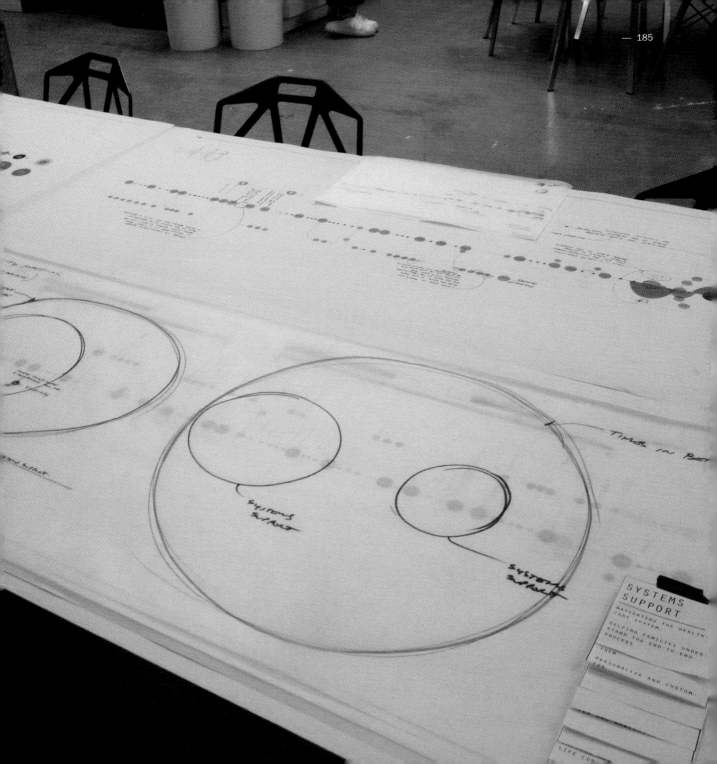

SYSTEMS
SUPPORT

NAVIGATING THE HEALTH
CARE SYSTEM

HELPING FAMILIES UNDER-
STAND THE END-TO-END
PROCESS

THEN
PERSONALIZE AND CUSTOM

HIRING DESIGN IS NOT ENOUGH WE NEED TO CR DESIGN THINKI

THINKERS

ATE

G COMPANIES.

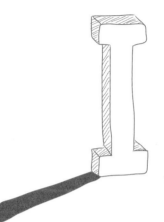

It is time to demystify what strategic planning is. Those are two separate things: strategy and planning. Planning is about analysis, and strategy is about synthesis. Planning is about facts, people, processes, operations, and finance budgets, whereas strategy requires creative thinking about customer needs, core capabilities, competition, and competitive advantage. Planning is a process approach to consider probabilities of what we think is going to happen and how it will happen, rather than consideration of the possibilities of what we want to happen or what we can make happen. Strategy is a process of continuous renewal and sense making that straddles the tension between competing for today and tomorrow; maintaining financial health and strategy health; and disrupting too much or not leveraging current core. Design thinking help leaders deal with these paradoxes and drive strategic dialogues and decisions around a new value system and tomorrow's possibilities.

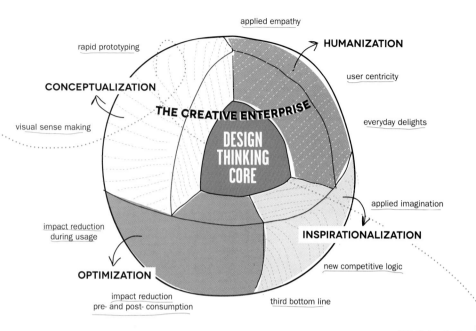

applied empathy

HUMANIZATION

rapid prototyping

CONCEPTUALIZATION

user centricity

THE CREATIVE ENTERPRISE

everyday delights

visual sense making

DESIGN THINKING CORE

applied imagination

impact reduction during usage

INSPIRATIONALIZATION

OPTIMIZATION

new competitive logic

impact reduction pre- and post- consumption

third bottom line

"THE COMPANIES THAT SURVIVE LONGEST ARE THE ONES THAT WORK OUT WHAT THEY UNIQUELY CAN GIVE TO THE WORLD—NOT JUST GROWTH OR MONEY BUT THEIR EXCELLENCE, THEIR RESPECT FOR OTHERS, OR THEIR ABILITY TO MAKE PEOPLE HAPPY. SOME CALL THOSE THINGS A SOUL."

—Charles Handy

Bill Gates is frustrated with our inability to improve the lives of the world's extremely poor. He believes that we can do better. He speaks of a new system that ties together capitalism's profit motive with the power of recognition. If we find "approaches that meet the needs of the poor in ways that generate profits and recognition for business," he says, "we will have found a sustainable way to reduce poverty in the world."

Gates and many other leaders believe business is the most powerful force for this global change. No other institution, including religions, governments, or nongovernmental organizations, has the resources, experience, or efficiency to deal with the most wicked social, environmental, educational, infrastructural, health, or financial challenges of today and tomorrow. To transform the world, however, business must first begin by transforming itself.

Jack Mackey, founder and co–chief executive officer (CEO) of Whole Foods, and his thought partner, Raj Sisodia, a business professor, wrote in their book *Conscious Capitalism* that capitalism can be a force both for economic and social good. And Bill George, former CEO of Medtronic, puts it in the book's introduction: "Well run, values-centered businesses can contribute to humankind in more tangible ways than any other organization in society."

That transformation is upon us. A generation of consumers who have grown up with the Internet and sharing through social media expect bigger and better things from their favorite brands. Richard Florida's "creative class" wants their employers to offer them real meaning and purpose in their work lives. The emergence of the B-corp has set new standards for how businesses operate. Everyone wants ingredients and behaviors to be healthier and more sustainable. And content—especially that which communicates who you are, what you believe in, and what you

are doing in the world—is once again king.

As this transformation gathers steam, the next generation of businesspeople can exert great influence and authority as they become leaders in their fields and usher in the age of creative capitalism—but only if they adapt and adopt ways of doing business that fulfill our expectations for positive change.

One of those ways will be to follow their intuition. In their seminal book *A Behavioral Theory of the Firm*, organizational theorists James March and Richard Cyert argue that intuition is critical to business success. They propose that managers treat intuition as real, memory as an enemy, experience as a theory, and the self as a hypothesis. Whatever the final decision, it should be, in part, driven by intuition. If this is not the case, then all business and strategy problems will continue to be solved by mathematicians and algorithms. Design thinking teaches us to bring intuition into the strategy process.

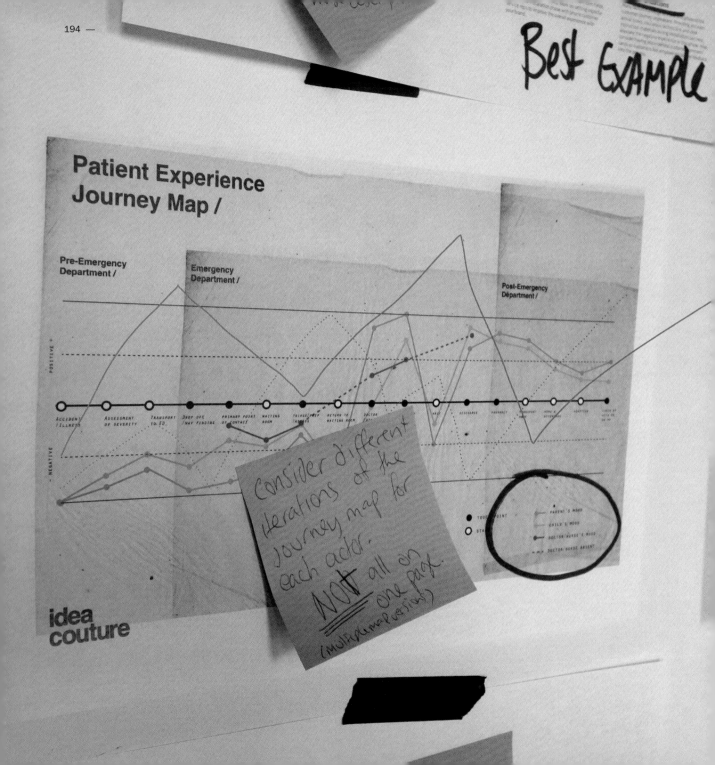

Minds are like parachutes; they only function when open.

—Thomas R. Dewar

Another way is for future business leaders to heed the power of the imagination. In "Theory Construction as Disciplined Imagination," organizational theorist Karl Weick suggests that strategists and others can increase their chances of success by stressing disciplined imagination. By *discipline*, he is simply referring to a balance to the wild side of fantasy. And by *imagination*, he is referring to the deliberate diversity of thought that is required to successfully formulate a problem, generate alternatives, and evaluate those alternatives. When conducted on an ongoing, disciplined basis, he argues that organizations will deliver better, truer results consistently. The idea is to balance logic with imagination—or teach designers to think like businesspeople and businesspeople to think like designers—design thinking is the most effective way to apply creative imagination to planning and strategy.

The Design Thinking Paradigm Change

Portfolio	*instead of*	**Planning**
Practice	*instead of*	**Theory**
Purpose	*instead of*	**Power**
System	*instead of*	**Objects**
Agility	*instead of*	**Structures**
Fast learning	*instead of*	**Formal education**
Rebellion	*instead of*	**Conformity**

THE TEST OF A FIRST-RATE INTELLIGENCE IS THE ABILITY TO HOLD TWO OPPOSED IDEAS IN THE MIND AT THE SAME TIME, AND STILL RETAIN THE ABILITY TO FUNCTION. ONE SHOULD, FOR EXAMPLE, BE ABLE TO SEE THAT THINGS ARE HOPELESS AND YET BE DETERMINED TO MAKE THEM OTHERWISE.

—F. Scott Fitzgerald

Yet another way is to look beyond the immediate ecosystems of the business world. The strategic planning model used by planning is essentially reductionist and limiting. By subdividing each part of a business into subparts and having teams organized around their own constituent parts, managers base their success on and develop their tactical plans to support those options that they have identified as being the most attractive and most actionable. The end result is that thousands of PowerPoint slides are circulated around the company that only speak to the company in the company's language. Design thinking can help managers think about wider systems, interdependencies, interconnectedness, and the patterns of behavior that are emerging in a world that will or will not eventually purchase your product based, largely, on those behaviors.

The idea of competitive advantage needs to be reconsidered in today's context. The assumption of sustainable competitive advantage is that it can be achieved at a steady state, and this thinking encourages all the wrong behaviors and reflexes that allow inertia to build up while business models become outdated. This results in denial rather than proactive participation in shaping the future.

And finally, the most important way for future business leaders to sustain performance is to adapt and adopt a human lens. The Industrial Revolution is over. The age of mass marketing is over. Even the age of globalization seems passé. Today and tomorrow are the first days in the age of kinship. We like. We share. We have friends. We link in. We invite. We endorse. We connect. Companies need to learn to do the same.

Design thinking is human-centric. It's by humans for humans. And its starting point might best be summed up by that great Charles Eames's quote, "Recognizing the need is the primary condition of design." Now more than ever, especially in this time of changes and crisis after crisis, business needs a human-centered approach to create real value for the people whose needs ultimately shape the size of its profits.

Imagine a business world shaped by intuition, imagination, interdependencies, and humanity. Those employees, managers, and executives who can balance and guide the data, metrics, analytics, strategy, and planning are real examples of Howard Gardner's synthesizing minds. Every team would be a multidisciplinary group made up of interdisciplinary people, or design thinkers.

That's a long way from where most companies are today. Although efficiency has been a key win of old-world disciplinary specialization, it has also been a curse. Organizational silos are everywhere, and many companies are on autopilot mode. They have separated people from each other's knowledge, created vocabularies that restrict real communication, put a damper on collaboration, cast creativity as crazy, and have opened the door for management consultants to pour in and propagate the status quo with their data, spreadsheets, and PowerPoint slides.

These problems are deep rooted in our school systems, including B-schools and D-schools. In B-schools around the world, professors are barely collaborating among themselves or with the outside the world of business, and the students coming out of their programs are exhibiting a serious creativity deficit. What's the problem?

Is it because our education systems have failed to produce enough businesspeople who are creative? Is it because creative people don't enroll in business school? Or is it because human resources departments fail to screen and hire their candidates for creativity?

In D-schools around the world, professors have little or no idea how business really works, and the students they are shepherding struggle to offer value to employers beyond their mechanical skills. What's the problem there? Is it because our education systems have failed to produce enough designers with analytical skills? Is it because analytical people don't enroll in design school? Or is it because human resources departments are afraid to hire creative, but qualified, people for analytical positions?

Ironically, almost everyone in both schools acknowledges that students should be taught in a more interdisciplinary fashion. Business schools such as Columbia and Yale have started to think differently. Columbia has set up two cross-disciplinary areas of research and teaching, one in decision and negotiation and the other in strategy. The same goes for some design schools. Parsons The New School for Design ran an MFA in Transdisciplinary Design that applies design thinking to study the intersection of cities, services, and ecosystems. Jamer Hunt will direct the new program to teach students to explore an impressive range of design problems, from reinvigorating the public sphere to fostering sustainable everyday practices. These are small steps. We need to see more happen in scale.

The challenges of the future will require multidisciplinary thinkers who will think first and work on solutions second. Today's layperson or specialist languages whether they are from the field of business, design, and engineering cannot properly describe who these people will be and what they will do. Ultimately, however, they will be synthesists. A design thinker is basically a synthesist, someone who possesses both analytical and emotional skills. This person's job is to pull together and integrate various disciplinary ideas, information, mental models, and methods and apply them to solving big problems.

Hiring people with these skills is not enough. Organizations need to have them built into their very DNA. If Bill Gates's call to action is to be realized, the B-schools and D-schools of the world need to be training and equipping young people with the skills that will be required to respond to challenges that transcend specialized disciplines.

Our graduates will have to develop a meta-knowledge of multiple disciplines and epistemologies. They must learn how to purposefully and reflectively integrate and synthesize different, often competing perspectives in order to deepen their understanding and effectively frame problems.

Rethinking traditional academic boundaries and traditional functional boundaries in large companies is an important mission. We know where we need to go. The challenges are monumental. But the transformations are critical. Now is the time to begin bridging the gaps between education and employment, between design and business, and between any of the remaining us and them that keeps us all from working together to unleash our imagination of a better future.

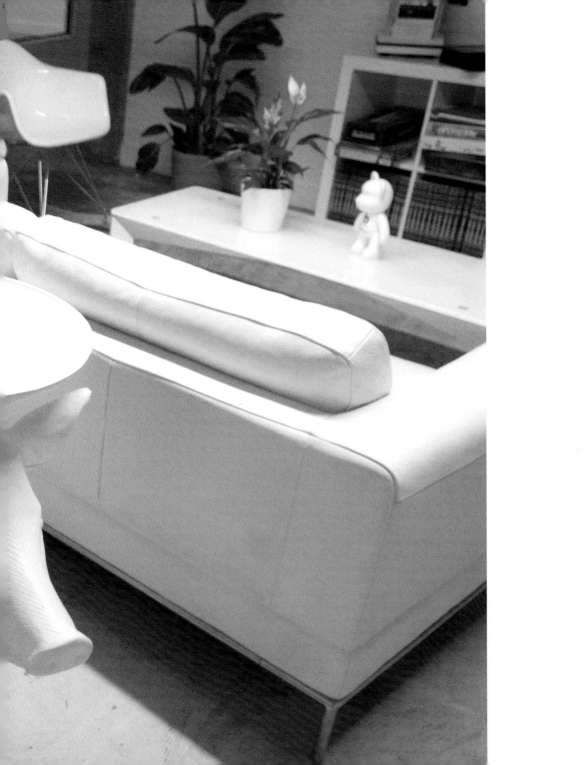

ABOUT THE AUTHOR

Idris Mootee is an authority in strategic innovation and applied design thinking in business strategy who has a long history of providing top executives with board-level strategic counsel and innovation guidance. Idris is currently the chief executive officer (CEO) of Idea Couture, a global strategic innovation firm with offices in London, San Francisco, Shanghai, Toronto, Mexico City, and Dubai, where he advises clients in different sectors to design innovation process, identify their highest-value innovation opportunities, and develop innovation capabilities. He designed and taught the Design Thinking for Business Innovation Executive Education Program at the Harvard Graduate School of Design and is a visiting professor at a number of business and design schools internationally. Idris speaks frequently at the world's most prestigious management conferences, and is a regular contributor to major media outlets.

PHOTO CREDITS

Special thanks to STUDIO O+A for use of photos on page 10–11, 23, 92–93, 106–107, 139, 146–147, 154–155, 186–187 by photographer Jasper Sanidad.

All other photos in this book are by Idris Mootee.

INDEX